S0-BZS-688

BESTSELLER

Must-Read
Author's
Guide to
Successfully
Selling Your Book

George Arnold

Illustrations by Jason C. Eckhardt

EAKIN PRESS ✺ Austin, Texas

Other Books by George Arnold
From Eakin Press

Growing Up Simple
A Nonfiction Novel
Foreword by Liz Carpenter

Coming Soon:

Los Cuatros Gatos Tejanos Les Salvan a Los Amigos Mexicanos
A Bilingual Adventure Novel

Typography and design by Amber Stanfield.

FIRST EDITION
Copyright © 2003
By George Arnold
Published in the United States of America
By Eakin Press
A Division of Sunbelt Media, Inc.
P.O. Drawer 90159 ⬤ Austin, Texas 78709-0159
email: sales@eakinpress.com
💻 website: www.eakinpress.com 💻
ALL RIGHTS RESERVED.
1 2 3 4 5 6 7 8 9
1-57168-799-8

Library of Congress Cataloging-in-Publication Data
Arnold, George, 1942-
    Bestseller: Must-read author's guide to successfully selling your book /
George Arnold.– 1st ed.
        p.   cm.
    Includes bibliographical references (p.)
    ISBN 1-57168-799-8 (alk. paper)
    1. Authorship–Marketing. I. Title
PN161.A77 2003
808'.02–dc21   2003008821

——This book is respectfully dedicated: ——

- to writers everywhere, whose urge to create defies reason, logic, and common-sense economics;
- to good publishers, who suffer incessantly from the barrage of demands from the aforementioned writers;
- to book retailers, whose Jobian patience is remarkable in the face of uninformed and downright naive expectations of those same writers.

Contents

So, You're an Author. Who Cares?

Oh, joy! Just what the world needs. Another how-to book for authors. The shelves of any decent-sized bookstore are already bulging with somebody or other's ideas of how to write, how to write better, how to be the best writer since God inscribed the tablets on Mount Sinai and sent Moses on back down to deliver the "Word." Why, you may ask, do I need the ideas and opinions of yet another guru? Especially one who never wrote a book until he was almost sixty years old?

Because this book is different. Because it makes a point the others have missed. The heart of the matter. The single element that separates the sheep from the goats when it comes to being a successful author.

That point?

Nothing happens until a sale is made.

I expect some of the greatest writers in history were never published. And some of the most talented writers of the last 200 years were published but remained completely obscure, going to their great rewards unknown. And penniless.

Why is that? Because as artists, as creators, as deep thinkers in some cases, they were never told the secret of being a successful author. That one ingredient they must bring to the party, or they will surely fail. Or, at best, remain obscure, undiscovered, penniless (at least as far as making money as a writer is concerned).

You are about to learn what a few authors have understood and been willing to do. You know them already: Mark Twain, Robert Ludlum, Patricia Cornwell, Stephen King, for heaven's sake. John Irving, Tom Clancy, Truman Capote, John Steinbeck, Ernest

Hemingway, Garrison Keillor, James Herriot. Add your own authors to this list. You could come up with maybe 100 names from the past 150 years.

"Well," you say, "these people are icons. They had natural talent. You can't expect everyone who writes to be a Shakespeare, can you? C'mon, now. Get real."

To which I, keeper of the secret heretofore, say: *Baloney.* Your entire list of 100 or so understood one thing that may never have crossed your mind. Or it may have crossed your mind, but it frightened you. Scared the living bejeezus right out of your creative psyche.

Admit it. I won't tell.

Yep. What those people knew and understood is that building a better mousetrap does not ensure the world will beat a path to your doorstep. Writing the great American novel, or any other brilliant work, is only the first part of the process. Mark Twain knew that. Stephen King knows that. So do Tom Clancy and a few dozen other authors, of varying quality as writers, I might add, who are perennial best-selling authors.

What's the point?

Here it is. Underline it. Put it on a three-by-five index card and slip it under your pillow and sleep on it:

> *You have to be willing, and that implies knowing how,*
> *to sell your book all by yourself. Because nobody else is*
> *going to do it for you.*

But, you say, what about my publisher and the bookstores? They have to sell the book. My only job is to write it.

Wrong! That's a great answer for *The Gong Show.* Never worked yet. Never will.

If you truly believe that, as apparently 99.44 percent of all authors do, then, my talented writer friend, you are doomed forever to obscurity. To be an unknown. Underappreciated. Misunderstood. A failure as a writer, at least economically speaking. And fame-wise, to be sure.

I can hear the retorts forming up in your gray matter, neurons firing at top speed, tongue poised to blurt forth, in utter defiance, "I can't do that! I'm a writer. An artist. A creator. An arranger of words in new and intriguing and interesting and funny and sad combinations. I don't know about selling. Besides, I'm a little shy and introverted anyway. Crowds scare me. I don't even like people much. Why can't the publishers and retailers just do their jobs and leave me to write?"

If you want to be *just* a writer, fine. Go write. Create to your heart's content. Knock out seventy-five thrill-packed pages a day. Every blessed day until the Armageddon.

Double-spaced, of course.

But if you expect anyone to ever read your writing, i.e., if you really want to be an *author,* cheer up. I'm here to tell you that you *can* do it. You *can* learn to sell your book. You can understand the process better—the roles of everybody involved in producing a product called a book.

Maybe you'll never be as successful as Robert Ludlum. Or as good a writer as John Irving. Or as flamboyant a character as Truman Capote. But there are more than 6.2 billion people on this planet. That's a bunch. And, as P.T. Barnum once observed, there are enough of them who will appreciate—maybe even *like,* your book, your style of writing, the subject matter you choose to write about—that you can sell a boatload of books. Enough, even, to maybe make a living as an author.

All you have to do is understand the roles. And learn to do your part. And sell.

That's what this book is about. To reveal to you, in the very simplest terms (because it is not complicated, and it's no deep-dark secret) what you need to do to become much more successful as an author. Be recognized at cocktail parties. Avoid bullies who kick sand into the faces of the unknowing on the beach. Attract the opposite sex.

Sounding better?

Yes, Virginia, there is a way. And we're going to explore it. Here and now.

Who Can Benefit from This Book?

I want to be up front with you. Although I earned part of my living, and a very good one, as a writer for more than thirty years, I was paid a salary for the writing and other chores I accomplished. My first published book crept out of obscurity when I had been retired several years and had reached the age of fifty-nine.

I had never written anything much longer than 200 words—the length of a sixty-second radio spot. Or a copy-heavy newspaper ad.

For forty years I had read between 125 and 160 books a year. An avid reader, you might say. Whenever I finished a book, about ninety percent of the time I would think to myself, and sometimes even say aloud, "I could do better than that."

After all, based on pure writing ability—the talent to make the language sing in brilliant word and phrase combinations—excellent writers are scarce as hen's teeth. Winston Churchill comes to mind as one who had the ability to use the language. Brilliantly. John Irving is in that same class, when it comes to fiction, in my estimation.

Speaking as a voracious reader, mind you. Not as a critic.

But of the best-selling authors—Ludlum, Clancy, Cornwell, King—none of them is truly a great writer. All are wonderful storytellers. Brilliant tale-spinners. But great writers?

I don't think so.

One night a couple of years ago, I had just finished the latest Ludlum tale. I'm an addict. A Ludlum lover. I put down the book, turned to my wife, and repeated my oft-thought opinion: "I could do better than that."

To my utter surprise, she challenged me. Not her style for the past forty years I have known her, but nevertheless, she looked at me with conviction and a bit of fire in her eyes (she's Italian) and said, "You always say that. Why don't you *do* it? And stop talking about it. *Capisce?*"

When she uses that word, she means business. I have learned, like Pavlov's dog, to either run for cover or do exactly what she has instructed. The proper (and only safe) response is, "*Capisco bene. Grazie.*" And then do it. Quick.

What the Sam Hill had I done? In the space of a few seconds, albeit with a forty-year overture, I had agreed with my *bella donna* to write a book.

Holy *frijoles!*

My education had been in journalism; my career in the marketing, advertising, and public relations business. As a writer, administrator, team leader. And agency president. To paraphrase Prissy in *Gone With the Wind,* "I didn't know nothin' 'bout birthin' no books."

So I turned to what I do know.

Marketing.

And to market successfully, one has to be able to communicate. To sell—both one-on-one and, by gentle persuasion, through impersonal vehicles. Like television, radio, newspapers, magazines. All the things we call media. One has to plan to work, and work a plan. Speaking tritely. But truthfully.

Perhaps, I thought (naively) I could apply the tools of marketing to the creation of a product. In this case, a book. It could happen. And it might even work. Besides, I didn't have any other better plan at the moment, and *la signora mia* was beginning to inquire, with alarmingly more frequent and pointed queries, concerning my progress.

Guess what? It worked!

And in the process, I have learned many things that will be helpful to authors. Most of whom, like me, are right-brained creators rather than analysts. Or bean counters, as we nonconformists like to call them.

So that is what this book is about: *the secrets of marketing applied to being a successfully selling author.*

What else is it?

Let's start with what it's not, so if you haven't already bought it, and you're looking for ways to use your word processing software more efficiently—and don't care a fig about selling more books— then you can avoid paying the $18.95. Plus tax.

What This Book Is Not

- A how-to-write-better guide. There is absolutely not a single word contained herein that will turn a bad writer into a better writer. Or a good writer into a great writer. Guaranteed. I wouldn't have a clue what to say on that subject.

  Except read. A lot.

- A detailed how-to-sell-your-manuscript-to-a-publisher guide. Well, we'll touch a bit on how to prepare better submissions and how to sell them, but only in the context of doing one's part in the entire process, rather than breaking in as a published writer. And not a word about agents—whether to use them or to avoid them. I readily admit ignorance on these subjects, having sold my first submission to the only publisher I submitted it to.

  Go ahead. Hate me. I can take it.

What This Book Is

- A thorough explanation, with real-life examples, of the roles that the writer, editor, book designer, publisher, and retail bookseller should play in the successful marketing of a book. The emphasis, of course, is on the writer's role at every step of the process.

- A step-by-step, and very simple, guide for the published author on what it takes to become a successful salesperson of one's own books.

- A practical and usable compendium of tips, tools, and suggestions for authors at every step of the process, from preparing a proper and appealing submission to actually selling your book at retail and by other means. Personal appearances. Speaking engagements. Events. Book clubs. Library gatherings. Trade shows.

Who Can Benefit from This Book?

- Published authors.
- Authors who want to be published.

- Authors willing to accept responsibility for selling their own books. It's not that hard. Really. We'll show you how.
- Booksellers whose Excedrin© headaches, caused by dealing with naive authors, are enough to drive them insane.
- Publishers whose time (half of it, anyway) is wasted by inexperienced authors who just don't know any better. Or those who just have bad business manners.
- Editors and book designers. To help them deal with authors more effectively. And save money on ammunition, perhaps.
- Teachers of writing and others in academia who work on that part of the process this book doesn't address—how to write. And write better.

There. See, I have just proved a point I made a few pages back.

In this world, there will always be enough people who will be interested in almost any book, which can, in turn, make that book an economic success.

If you—the author—have learned how to be a bestseller, that is. Just remember: *Nothing happens 'til a sale is made.*

GEORGE ARNOLD
Fredericksburg, Texas
2003

Part I

In the Beginning . . .

Chapter 1

Why? Why? Why Do I Write?

Okay, here's the drill. Stand in front of a mirror. Grab onto big globs of your hair with both hands. Pull it up and outward until it really hurts, all the while repeating the title of this chapter.

Got it?

Go ahead. I'll wait.

Fun, wasn't it? And I'll bet you've already done this at least a thousand times. In frustration. Anger. When writer's block has you firmly by the throat. And you're really not capable of doing much else.

So, what's the answer? Why do we do it?

Every writer, if he or she is honest with him- or herself—very hard to do, especially when analyzing irrational actions—has a complex set of answers to the question. Most of which don't make sense anyway.

Is it for the money? Probably not, unless you've figured out how to live on $600 a year. Net, of course.

For the glory? That's a laugh. The fraction of all authors who become famous is smaller than the percentage of impurities in Ivory Soap. About half of one percent.

Because we don't know how to do anything else? Likely not, since most of us have day jobs anyway, and have learned to live on four hours of sleep. So we can write half the night.

In my case, I do it because my wife told me to. I'm afraid of her. Always have been. Better safe than sorry, you know.

Whatever your individual complex matrix of answers may be, we all likely share a common thread. And we're victims of that thread. We are driven to create. It's like an ugly gene that takes over our brains, our keyboards, our screens and printers. And it says to all of us, "Write. Or I'll kill you. Tie you to a tree in Baghdad and send your photo and location to Osama bin Laden."

Doesn't matter whether we have any real writing skills or not. "It" doesn't care that we don't know a plot from Shinola. Or a compound-complex sentence from an adverbial phrase.

We have to do it. There is no choice.

Fortunately, a certain small segment of hominids has been driven to create through writing from the beginning of recorded history. How else do you think it got "recorded"?

Picture this. The year is 24,000 B.C. Of course, nobody knew it was B.C. Because there was no C yet. But I digress. We are in the mouth of a cave in northern China. Or Central Africa. Mesopotamia, even. Doesn't matter.

A hairy biped named Conk is furiously scraping away at the south wall of the cave with a large rock he's already chipped to flatness on one side. He's preparing a "canvas" for his friend, Grog, who is—also furiously—pounding leaves and herbs and all sorts of vegetable and animal matter into colorful little piles on the cave's floor.

Conk and Grog might just have been the Rodgers and Hammerstein of 24,000 B.C. Conk, the assistant, is preparing the surface so that Grog, the creative writer, can commence to put up a message. In pictures and symbols that will be generally understood by the residents of the immediate area.

This morning, Grog has decided to write a humorous short story. Remember that marking on a cave wall is a process that doesn't lend itself too well to the production of epics. Especially when the average life span is only nineteen years.

Conk's and Grog's wives are nagging them. "You guys are a pain in the gluteus maximus. Do you know that? Hey! I'm talking to you. Yes, both of you. Why can't you be like everybody else and get a job? Go pick gooseberries for a pie? Or kill a wooly mammoth, skin him, and dry his flesh so we can eat next winter? But, noooo. Not you two louts. You've just got to mess up the walls with your scribbling. We should've married traveling Tartars. At least they don't decorate their skin-tents with silly-ass scribbles!"

Cut to 2003 A.D. Now you know it's A.D. And you're at your keyboard, trying desperately to come up with a coherent sentence or two. It's 2:00 A.M. Your wife stumbles in, a ratty robe hastily wrapped around her, her hair a mess and eyes blinking. She puts her hands on her hips and says something like this to you.

"Are you still pecking away at that damned keyboard? You better go to bed and get some sleep. You have to go to work in the morning and try to do a day's work. I'm afraid this writing nonsense is going to cost you your job and us our house and self-respect. Are you listening to me, Grog? Oh, what the hell! You're hopeless!"

The more things change, the more they stay the same. Right?

From the beginning of time, those driven to be creative have been labeled as quasi-perverts by the clueless masses who have not a whit of creativity, or appreciation for creativity, in their bodies.

Think it was easy being Dante? He was driven out of his city-state by the woman he loved because he dared to try to be creative. And you can be sure he achieved little money, glory, fame, or appreciation before he was long dead.

Same for Leonardo and Michelangelo. And Shakespeare. They had to scrabble, practically sell their souls, to come up with "sponsors" who would underwrite some of the most creative works in man's history.

The point of this little journey down history lane is simple. It's not easy to be a creative person. Never has been. Maybe never will be.

Our "modern" education system, which hasn't changed much in the last 500 years (rows of desks, teachers in front, blackboards behind the teachers) does its best to beat the creativity out of every candidate graduating from kindergarten to the first grade.

"Color inside the lines! Don't just scribble! You can do better than that. And use your right hand, for heaven's sake. You'll be miserable left-handed in a right-handed world."

Scribbling is gut-level creativity. Especially for a five-year-old. But very few appreciate that. Little left-handed, right-brained Johnny in the twenty-first century will suffer the same slings and arrows of outrageous ostracism that bedeviled Shakespeare and Einstein, Leonardo and Michelangelo. Only Little Johnny probably doesn't have the "go to hell" genes to tell his critics to piss off—that he's going to scribble one color on top of the other until he, himself, is satisfied with what he's created.

So, throughout history, there have been few Einsteins or Shakespeares. Or Leonardos. Or Michelangelos. Or Dantes.

As long as we, who are driven to create, don't think about why we do what we do, and can't succinctly verbalize to the analytical, left-brained noncreatives the importance of what we do, there will continue to be few of us who do gain financial reward and personal recognition.

That's the way it is. The way it has forever been. I mention it early in this book so you will have plenty of time to think about it and what it means to you.

Given that affliction, which we all share, the question is not "How do we overcome the urge?" Why should we? It's our right. Our quest. No, the real questions are these: How do we

- make some money—real money?
- stand proud in the face of rejection?
- avoid as much of that rejection as possible?
- create books that will sell?
- and actually have fun in the whole process?

Those are some of the things we're going to be exploring in the pages ahead. I warn you now: If you're into masochism and self-fla-gellation, you're not going to like what we're about to uncover. The emphasis will be on fun. Personal fun for the author, the publisher, the editor, and book designer. And for the retailers in the sales chain, as well as the ultimate consumers of your work.

Mini Thought-Starters

Humor—Can you think of anything much worse than something that's supposed to be humorous but isn't? Talk about falling flat. Here's a simple way to judge if something is really funny:

Humor has two parts, or elements. First, it must be innocent. That is, there is no intended harm to anybody in its content. Second, it must appear to be spontaneous—unexpected. That's why little kids are so funny. They are innocent. And they are spontaneous in a to-tally uninhibited way.

Creativity—What constitutes creativity? Stripped down to its basics, creativity is the result of taking a totally uninhibited look at a subject from a completely unexpected, even unorthodox, viewpoint. Followed by the fearlessness to record that look and show it to others.

It was Mark Twain who observed there's really nothing new under the sun—just new ways of looking at old things. That's a pretty good definition of creativity from the writer who perfected the art form known as the American novel.

Why?
Why?
Why do I write?

Chapter 2

What, Exactly,
Have You Created?

Sitting in my publisher's lobby one day, I was surprised to hear an author presenting his manuscript actually say something like this: "I'm not sure who the target for this book will be. Maybe women will like it more than men. I just don't know."

When he had finished his business and left, and it was my turn to meet with the editorial and production staff, I asked about what I had overheard. "Oh, yes," I was absolutely assured, "lots of authors finish a manuscript without ever giving any definitive thought to who the audience for the book really will be. Just as often, they have an absolutely definite idea that's totally wrong."

Apparently it's an occupational quirk among authors. Wouldn't work for Procter & Gamble. Or General Motors. Or Sony. Every major producer of consumer products knows precisely who their product will appeal to before they ever give a thought to producing large quantities and unleashing it on the masses. Yet still, a high percentage of new products fail in the marketplace.

I wondered, "What chance does an author have producing a book with no idea whatsoever (or even worse, a completely wrong idea) about who might be interested in the subject matter?"

Not much.

Then I wondered, "How can a book designer come up with an appropriate 'look' for a product that might be for young women? Or maybe for left-handed Irishmen with handlebar mustaches who live in manufactured housing west of the Mississippi River and south of Fargo, North Dakota?"

No way. Can't be done.

"What about the editor?" I continued thinking. To myself, of course. Seems everybody else in the room already knew about these giant potholes in the road to producing a book. I was just learning something almost everybody else seemed to know. I say "almost" everybody else because it was becoming pretty clear to me (takes me a while, but then I catch on fast) that way too many authors don't seem to know they have a problem.

Well, it was all pretty amazing to me. Especially when it's not a very difficult problem to overcome. And, in the process, defining the new book's potential audience can give it about a ten-thousand-times-better chance to be a success.

Motorola knows how to do it. So does Ford. Sure, there's an occasional Edsel. Or "New" Coke. But such marketing gaffes are few and far between, and you haven't seen a big one lately. Have you?

Once again, the answer is terribly simple. Didn't I promise it was not going to be complicated?

The introduction of every product is preceded by something called *research*. And guess what? You can do it, too. Just like General Mills does it. And, as a result, you will know with certainty who your manuscript will appeal to.

Before the editor has to make judgments.

Before the book designer has to decide whether to make it look rustic or frilly.

Before the promotions department has to produce a pre-publication flyer announcing your new book. Or decide who ought to receive that flyer.

The net result? Your book will get off to a decent start and have a much better chance of being successful.

Before you tell me that Quaker Oats spends $20 million researching a new product and you don't have those kinds of resources, let me quickly point out that Quaker Oats has a whole lot more at stake than you have. Their $20 million expenditure to find out all about their new product may save them a $250 million failure. Sure, they spend mega-bucks. But all things are relative.

For a very few hours of your time (compared to the time you've spent on your manuscript) and a very few out-of-pocket dollars, you can enhance your chances of success geometrically. In fact, I would go so far as to say that less than a $100 investment will give you all the answers you need to position your book accurately and appropriately. And look (and be) smart in the process.

Would you pay $100 to ensure your book has the best chance possible to sell well? Sure you would.

Then do it.

What are some of the things you can learn from some very simple, inexpensive research? How about these:

- Is your book's primary appeal to men? Women? Children? Or nobody?
- Does it seem to deliver any regional biases (e.g., Southerners hate it)?
- Do readers find the book interesting? How interesting?
- Do readers find the book informative? How informative?
- Do readers think it's funny? Sad? Hilarious? Disgusting?
- To what degree does a cross-section of readers appreciate it?
- How much would consumers be willing to pay for it?
- What other books and authors' styles do readers think it resembles?
- Is it long enough? Too long? Just right?
- Would readers like to read more books by you?

The list of attributes and characteristics, strengths and weaknesses you can uncover about your book *before you finish your own edit of the manuscript* is formidable. And easy (there's that word again) to get to.

Before we go any further, I want to be sure you're with me. That you believe, as I do, that a little extra effort upfront is worthwhile.

Consider two simple scenarios. You are the central focus of both.

Scenario one: You hand-deliver your completed manuscript to your publisher and meet with your assigned editor and book designer. The publisher's sales department is also represented. Everybody is excited at this milestone meeting. It's your turn to present your work. So you look around the room, lift the box of 750 pages, and set it tenderly on the conference room table. You begin to speak: "Well, here it is. One hundred twenty-five thousand words. Twenty-four chapters. I call it *Devil's Lust in the Dust Devils.* I sure hope you like it and somebody buys it. I wrote it to appeal to women in their twenties, but I think a lot of other people might like it, too. Even a few men."

Scenario two: Same situation. Same people present. You set your manuscript on the table and begin to speak: "This is a romance novel set in the 1890s. Its primary appeal seems to be to women under fifty, although there's a secondary market among men over sixty-five. Readers tend to consider it very realistic in its story line, and they give the dialogue high marks for believability. At 125,000 words, I think it should sell for about $24.95 at retail, although a cross-section of readers indicated they would pay anywhere from $20 to $30 for it. There seems to be no consensus as to price point, so that probably needs more study. Here's a complete research report that will be helpful to you, Amber, as you do the design and especially to you, Melissa, as you begin to edit. I have some thoughts for the dust cover design I'd like to discuss—when it's time, of course, and based on some pretty spectacular verbatim quotes I got from some individual readers who checked out the manuscript for me.

"You know what? This thing kinda fooled me. I thought all along that the appeal to women would be strong, but the business of men over sixty-five liking it and finding it interesting and informative just blew me away. Proves, I guess, we can't rely on our own ideas—even instincts. We're just too close to the product to be objective."

Bingo!

Which scenario appeals to you the most?

If you picked the first scenario, take this book right back to the store and see if they will give you your money back. It's not going to help you to finish it. You're just out $18.95. Plus tax, of course.

I suspect most readers would like to see themselves in the second scenario. So let's talk a bit about what you can do, easily and inexpensively, to get yourself into that picture. And never have to stumble through a meeting like scenario one. Ever.

Besides, I promise you several things: Your editor will love you. Your book designer will love you. Your publisher's sales department will love you. And when they all love you, guess what? You get their full attention. Best talent. Strongest efforts.

The reasons are simple. You've not wasted their time. And time is money. You've made it exponentially easier for them to do their jobs for you. Better than they will ever be able to do them for the bozo in scenario one. Even if they wanted to be nice to the bozo.

Which they won't. Trust me.

By now, I hope you're convinced. So it's time to show you just how easily and inexpensively you can understand your product, fairly exactly, and give yourself a leg up on both your fellow authors and on introducing a successful book. And remember, I promised you won't spend more than $100 doing it. Plus a few hours of your time.

Here's how.

Step one: Once you have completed your comprehensive outline, and even before you begin to write the text, take a day off and organize your own reader panel. This reader panel should consist of a minimum of twenty persons, up to as many as thirty-six. Try for an even mix of males and females, if possible. Select people from various parts of the country, and do your best to have the following age groups more or less equally represented: eighteen to twenty-four; twenty-five to forty-nine; fifty to sixty-five; over sixty-five. Of course, if you are writing a children's book or a juvenile book, select an equal number of appropriately aged children and their parents.

This is critically important: *Be sure to select only people who will level with you. Those you know will say only nice things and just patronize you will ruin the effort.*

Simply contact these people (e-mail is a quick and yet personal way to round up a group of volunteers in a hurry). If you want thirty readers, recruit thirty-two. Invariably a couple of well-meaning souls will volunteer and then get too busy to follow through.

Don't be bashful. Most people will consider it fun and a bit of a privilege to be involved in the birthing of a new book.

Once you have your panel selected, simply e-mail them the draft of each chapter as you complete its first edit—your edit. Ask them to read it and send back any thoughts or suggestions they may have. Do not be specific about the kind of feedback you want. That comes later. Just let them react.

You'll be amazed at the amount of useful feedback that will be returned. Great ideas for improving the manuscript, as well as minuscule details and factual corrections—all of which will make your book better.

I recommend you take the feedback seriously and remember not to have your feelings hurt when your favorite sentence seems to be a bummer to half of them. Just chalk it up to false pride of authorship. And fix it.

At the rate of a chapter every five or six days, this process will consume several months. But it won't take any more time than good writing, in a vacuum and without feedback, would take. By the time you've sent out the last chapter, you'll find yourself way ahead in the game.

Step two: Once you have incorporated all the changes and corrections you consider helpful, then send each reader a simple questionnaire. About a dozen semantic-differential scaled questions will give you an excellent read. You know—the kind of questions that have something like "ugly" on the left extreme and "gorgeous" at the other extreme. With five or seven little equal spaces between for you to register the intensity of your opinion. (See Exhibit A at the end of this chapter.)

Be sure to include a couple of open-ended questions, too, so your readers can say things to you that may not be covered in your questions. This whole process can be completed by e-mail.

For an example of a real questionnaire that was used to help make a decent manuscript much, much better, see Exhibit B, immediately following this chapter and in the Appendix. Look at the kinds of questions that were asked, and note that the verbatim responses were actually used on the first edition's dust cover. And in the author's press kit. And on other promotional material.

Bottom line: This author knew what a variety of readers thought about his manuscript, who the book would appeal to, what other works the book was considered comparable to, how much—approximately—readers said they would be willing to pay at retail. In short, a wealth of information that made his meeting with the publisher's staff—his real-life scenario—rewarding and refreshing to everyone in the room.

Note also, in the author's analysis of the research results, the number of times he expresses surprise at the answers, proving that writers may very well be the worst judges of the products they produce.

Step three: Research sometimes plays tricks. Unlike the clarity exhibited in the sample questionnaire, suppose an area or two were somewhat ambiguous. If so, step three would be to pick up the phone and have a one-on-one discussion with several of the people whose views were so divergent as to cause this confusion or ambiguity. Or maybe, like the results in the example, yours will be so clear that you won't even have to spend any money on long distance.

There it is. In the now-famous words of Porky Pig, "Th-th-th-that's all, folks!"

Two steps, for sure. Maybe three. A few hours of organization time. A few more of analysis and think time.

And, end results?

You know, pretty darn precisely, what kind of a product you've created, how to position it in the marketplace, and to whom it is really aimed. And the manuscript will be better than if you holed up in a garret somewhere and shared it with nobody.

Guaranteed.

And all for less than $100 out of your pocket.

Oh, one more thought. Be a thoughtful person and send each of your reader panel members both a copy of the final research report and a signed, personalized first edition as soon as it's available. You owe them more than they'll ever realize. But you can make them feel good with an e-mailed research report and a book that'll cost you less than $10.

Wholesale, of course. But you don't have to tell them that.

Exhibit A. Sample Semantic-Differential Scale Questions

:	:	:	:	:	:	:	:
Gorgeous	Pretty	Lovely	Neutral	Homely	Ugly	Grotesque	

:	:	:	:	:	:	:	:
White Hot	Red Hot	Warm	Ambient Temp.	Cool	Cold	Ice Cold	

:	:	:	:	:	:	:	:
Hilarious	Funny	Humorous	Neutral	Sad	Very Sad	Depressing	

Exhibit B. Actual Research Results Report

2. *I found the book to be:*	Female Respondents	Male Respondents	Total
Extremely interesting	7	3	10
Very interesting	5	6	11
Somewhat interesting	-	-	-
No opinion	-	-	-
Somewhat uninteresting	-	-	-
Very uninteresting	-	-	-
Extremely uninteresting	-	-	-
Totals	**12**	**9**	**21**

Analysis: Clearly, the book is considered quite interesting, again with females ranking it slightly higher than males. Note that the responses are identical to question one, although individual responses are not identical.

3. *For me, the book was:*	Female Respondents	Male Respondents	Total
Extremely entertaining	8	4	12
Very entertaining	4	5	9
Somewhat entertaining	-	-	-
No opinion	1	-	1
A little bit boring	-	-	-
Very boring	-	-	-
Extremely boring	-	-	-
Totals	**13**	**9**	**22**

Analysis: The positive trend continues, as does the trend toward slightly higher rankings by women than men. Respondents found the book highly entertaining. The one "no opinion" notation was actually just left blank, entirely.

Comment: The primary intent of the book, from the author's point-of-view, is to entertain. Apparently it has succeeded. The combination of high marks for entertainment, interest, and positive-reaction is heartening.

Above is a sample from an actual research results report. To see the entire report, refer to the Appendix at the conclusion of this book.

Chapter 3

Are We Having Fun Yet?

You still with me? Good.

So far, we've taken a look at what drives us to create and how to objectively "get smart" about our manuscripts and their real target audiences.

I hope you're not discouraged. Because, if we can't have fun doing what we seem to be driven to do, why even do it? Masochism, maybe? After all, and I know you don't want to hear this (but it's required, like a dose of caster oil), the likelihood of becoming rich and famous is minuscule, although some of you will. The chance to even make a decent living is pretty small. But some of you will. And your chances will be enhanced, dramatically, if you'll read on and pay attention to what I'm telling you.

And act. As Nike says, "Just do it."

So, let's at least have some fun at it.

Things we do or have to do from time to time that are not fun mostly involve doing the unknown. Right? The first time we have to do anything is pretty scary. Or at least not a lot of fun. Like parachuting out of a perfectly good airplane. Just as an example, don't you see?

As we move forward through this little epistle, I promise you that I will do my best to show you how easy it is to do the things you've never done before, but which you absolutely *must* do if your book is

16

going to be a sales success. My hope is that, once you see how it's done (and how simple it is), you can approach your expanded role in the marketing of your book with the anticipation of enjoying the process—*actually having some fun.*

If you read the trade press even occasionally, you already know that publishers (even the mega-houses) no longer are willing, for sure, or able, so they say, to provide the promotional support they used to provide as a matter of course. If you're working with a smaller, regional publisher (and there aren't many of them left), you may even get more marketing support than with one of the biggies. If you are self-publishing, what follows is even more critical—because you're all alone out there. With only your wits (and this little guide) to fend off all the forces that will try to do you in. Incessantly. Every day.

Of course, if you're Clancy or King or Irving, you'll need less of an effort. But I seriously doubt those guys are reading this book. (Hey, if you are, let me know. I'll autograph it for you. Even send you one for free. Heh-heh.)

Fact is, even the lexicon is changing, and those changes are a clear reflection of the attitude behind the words. For example, notice that publishers are now referring to authors as *"content providers"*? And manuscripts as *"content"*?

What does that tell you?

Probably that there are so many authors producing so many manuscripts that both the writer and the written have become commodities.

Soap powder. Corn flakes. Enriched flour. Cornmeal.

If you find that distressing, or off-putting, or maybe even scary, have no fear, my creative friend. Do not *Tide* and *Kellogg's* and *Aunt Jemima* and *Quaker Oats* manage to differentiate and promote their particular brands (of what are truly commodities) as "different and better"?

The process is called "branding," and you can do it for your book. And for yourself.

In fact, if you expect to have a prayer of selling many books, you HAVE to do it. Branding, that is.

As we move on through the chapters that follow, I'll show you how. Step by step. One. Two. Three. You think maybe the marketing director of Procter & Gamble's Tide brand is smarter than you? Not likely. He just knows something already that you don't yet know. But I know it, too. And I'll let you in on it.

Result: You can make yourself and your book (even though both of you may be just "average" — a couple of commodities) stand out from the crowd as "different and better."

"So, what's he saying here, Mabel? That I, the author, the creator, the brains and talent behind this book, also have to become the marketer and the salesman?"

"Sounds like it to me, Fred."

"Can I do that, Mabel?"

"I guess you'd better, Fred."

I guess you'd better, Fred. I know you have to, Freida. There is no longer a choice, Elwood.

So, let's get to it.

In this chapter, just to put your mind at ease, we're going to take an overview look at some of the tools and concepts you'll need to create and employ to make yourself and your book "different and better."

In later chapters (Part IV), we'll get into how to create those tools and concepts, how to use them as part of a devilishly clever plan which you, yourself, will concoct and put into place.

Really.

For now, though, let's just look at some of the things you must do and some of the tools you'll need to do them.

The Author's Role

If you are now going to become your own marketing guru, salesman and promoter, just what is it you'll have to learn how to do?

Here it is. This may not be an exhaustive list, but it's enough to get the job done. You, creative person that you are, will be able to enhance it without help from anybody. Once you commit to coming to the party.

Things an author, today, must be able and willing to do. And look forward to doing. And have fun doing.

- Form your own reader panel and conduct the research necessary to enable you to be "smart" about your book and its most likely target audiences.

- Using that knowledge, sell your manuscript to a publisher.
- "Brand" both yourself and your book as different and better than the hundreds, if not tens of thousands, of other authors and books you'll be competing with in the marketplace.
- Promote your "brands" (yourself and your book) to get them noticed. To generate interest in them. To move beyond total obscurity as an author and a book.
- Participate mightily in the effort to sell your book into the retail trade. That will mean calling on the area marketing managers and community relations managers and store managers of chain booksellers and independent bookstores, providing promotional samples and convincing them you can make them some money.
- Schedule your own appearances—both at bookstore signings and at events where you will find a lot of the people who represent your book's target audience.
- Learn to sell your book, one-on-one, assertively (without being aggressive) on the retail sales floor and at the aforementioned events.
- Create a *persona,* a character—if you will—that you can and must assume to be more successful at these selling opportunities. It's your *brand.* Like Mr. Whipple. Or Mrs. Olsen. Or Tony the Tiger.
- Become a hard-nosed, disciplined recordkeeper.
- Follow up, follow up, follow up. Then follow up. And follow up again.

Do those look like things you can do? Do you want to do them? Will you resolve to have fun doing them?

If your answer to these questions is consistently "no," maybe you ought to find another avocation. Because being a successful author is not a hobby. Can't be. Won't work. Never has. Never will.

If your answer to the first question (can do?) is "no," but you're willing to assign a "yes" to questions two and three (want to and have fun), then read on. I can show you how to do them. But I can't give you the "want-to." I can show you how the whole magilla can be fun, if you will let it. But I can't change your mindset from misery or drudgery to "Yahoo!"

Tools You'll Use. Really Use.

Now that you have an idea of the role you must play to be a "best-selling author," at least in general terms, what are some of the aids and tools you'll need to create to help you along with that process?

Here is a list of the most significant items. Again, as with your role, you may discover other ideas that will be beneficial, too. In fact, if you don't, you're not thinking. Hard enough, anyway.

- A complete research report.
- A complete, and attractive, press kit. Contents? Synopsis of the book; one-page bio of the author; news release about the book; short feature story related to one of the main aspects of the book; photo of the author; promotional sample of the book. Signed and personalized, for sure.
- Point-of-sale material. Primarily posters and shelf-talkers (thin strips that attach to the shelves under your books). Your publisher will help you with these.
- A pre-publication announcement mailer with order forms. Again, your publisher will assist.
- A signing and event kit. We'll get into all the things you'll need to bring along to a signing later, in Chapter 10.
- Promotional mailing and contact lists. Lots of lists. Book editors. Book reviewers. Talk show producers. Bookstore managers. Book chain area marketing managers and community relations managers. Start in the cities in your immediate vicinity, and then work outward as you go.
- Invitation mailing lists and postcard invitations to signings. A list of friends, acquaintances, target audience influencers. At least fifty people for each market you will target for signings and event appearances. Your publisher will help you with the postcard invitations, but you will have to create the lists on databases. Avery © brand labels work great!
- Checklists, with follow-up built in.
- Schedules, with flexibility to change. Hourly.
- Computerized records. Of sales by distribution channels; i.e., direct from publisher, book retailers, personal sales at events, comp copies. (We'll talk about the importance of personal recordkeeping in Chapter 9.)

Are you beginning to get the idea that writing the book might be the easy part? Good. It probably is easier at this point. Because you know how to do that, and the rest of this stuff is still a bit foreign.

That's okay. You're right where you ought to be at this point.

So try not to worry about any of these things. You will see that they're not so difficult, after all. We'll have you self-promoting with the best in a few more chapters.

And selling more books.

And having more fun.

As the software salesman said, "Trust me."

———— Part II ————

There Was a Manuscript.

Chapter 4

The Dreaded Submission– Make It Count.

Most of us who are driven to create through the written word will push ourselves until we have at least the first draft of a semi-finished product. Something we lovingly call a "manuscript."

We sit back, thumb through it admiringly, and imagine it transformed, as if by magic, into a completed product—a real book.

But something's missing here. We have a story on paper. But who's going to turn it into that real book?

With any luck, the answer is a real publisher. But something's still missing here. We have to sell the book to a real publisher. How do we do that?

The actual sales process begins with research, as we have previously noted. Then we need to figure out how to make the book as attractive to publishers as possible. And which publishers we need to approach.

Many authors will prepare a submission (sample of the book) and send it to several publishers simultaneously. Like throwing a pot full of stuff against a wall in the hope that some of it will stick.

Wrong. Bad idea. Almost certain to create a "Teflon" © effect, which will result in everything sliding down the wall and making a mess on the floor. So to speak.

"Okay, wise guy," you're saying to me, albeit silently, "do you know a better way?"

Indeed, I do.

And here it is.

After your research is complete and you're "smart" about your product and the target audiences it will likely appeal to, the first thing you need to do is . . . some more research.

Really.

The purpose of this research (simple inquiries, actually) is to determine which publishers have a propensity to accept (read "buy" and publish and distribute) books that are similar to yours. If your book is *Devil's Lust in the Dust Devils,* for example, it's highly unlikely that the Christian Word Publishing Company is going to have an interest in it—except, perhaps, to suggest it be banned. Or burned.

Now, that's an absurd example, of course. On the other hand, publishers of nonfiction history tell me they get adventure novel submissions every week. Total waste.

How do you narrow your target publishers to those most likely to have an interest in the subject you're trying to sell? Same way you would for any other product that needs to be sold. If you're selling hamburger buns, the local five-and-dime store is most likely not interested. Better to approach Mom's Diner, don't you think?

A world of information about publishers is available on the Internet. Just crank up a trusty search engine or two and do a quick inventory of publishers' Web sites. The home page of each publisher's site will almost invariably tell you—or at least give you a clue—as to the kinds of books that publishing house is interested in. In a couple of hours, you can find a dozen potential publishers who might have an interest in *Devil's Lust in the Dust Devils.*

Now you can whip up a nifty submission package and fire it off to all of them.

Right?

Wrong again.

I know you don't want to hear this, because it means additional work. I promised you it would be fun (or could be fun, if you let it), but I didn't say that some effort wouldn't be required. Did I?

Go back to each of those home pages and click on the icon labeled "Submissions." In each case, I promise—cross my heart—that publisher will tell you, precisely, in what form they expect to receive submissions.

Listen closely. This is critical: Tailor your submissions to each publisher's specifications. Exactly. No fudging allowed. Generic submissions don't count. Might as well toss that package into a well and forget about it.

Why is this so important?

Two reasons: First, it tells the publisher, right off the bat, that you are the kind of author who cares about their needs, can follow directions, and listen when they need to tell you something. If you don't fit that mold, right out of the chute, why should they even fool with looking at your work? I don't care how great it is, an author who appears oblivious or uncaring goes to the end of the line. Or in the trash, more likely.

Being able and willing to supply precisely what they prescribe tells publishers they can expect both a clean, easy-to-work-with manuscript and a willing-to-learn, easy-to-work-with author.

The second reason to customize those submissions precisely for each publisher is that they will actually look at submissions that meet their specs. They will set aside those that don't.

Yes, they will. And they will probably never get back to the "can't follow directions" stack. They're busy. And they have their reasons for wanting submissions in their formats.

Again, like Nike, just do it.

Does that mean you have to create a dozen separate submissions to approach twelve different publishers? Not really. It does mean that you have to use your computer or word processor to format what is essentially the same submission in many different ways. But that won't take long. And it won't be difficult.

You can do it. I have faith.

You have to do it. Or be ignored.

So, now you have all your submissions formatted, customized, and ready to go. Right?

Not just yet.

Remember that each publisher has given you a roadmap for submissions. You have followed it. Precisely. And that will put you ahead of all those who don't know enough or care enough to follow directions.

Next question is: "How can you get from the 'acceptable format' stack to the head of the class?" That's your new objective, isn't it? To rise to the top of the stack at the publisher's weekly submission review session? You want to be the one or two authors whose submissions get past the first screening and into the "further investigation" file.

How do you do that? This gets really easy. Remember your research report? Now's the first time to pull it out and start to demonstrate your "smarts." Do not include the entire report with your initial submission. It's too much. Looks too formidable to have to wade through.

But do include two or three sample questions, with results, to show what you have already done. And refer to it in your cover letter. Tell the publisher that you already know your book will appeal to women between twenty-five and forty-nine and to men over sixty-five. Allude to the fact that you have done extensive research, and you already know not only what kind of product you have created but also who will likely buy it and how much they have already said they would be willing to pay for it. Don't quote sales prices. Just let them know that you have some information that will aid in setting the retail price.

"Cancel this week's submissions review meeting. None of these bozos can even follow directions!"

Much of this can be told in a cover letter. No more than two pages. "Any other tips?" I can hear you asking.

Here's one that worked for me when I began to prepare to sell my first book. I brazenly asked a famous person who is a well-known writer, among other talents, to write the foreword for my book.

Guess what? She agreed.

So I could tell the prospective publisher that, even though this is my first book and nobody had ever heard of me as an author, a well-known writer and public personality has already agreed to participate in my project, thus giving it two advantages: name recognition for the cover (to enhance sales potential); and the implied endorsement of someone who is generally recognized as knowing the difference between bullion and bull.

Here's the point: Give yourself every advantage. Position your product and yourself as easy to work with and sure to help the publisher make some money. That's the bottom line for the publisher, after all—making a profit and avoiding working with amateurs or prima donnas.

Pre-Submission Checklist

Okay, let's review. When you start to put together submissions, here are the rules to maximize your chances for success:

- Research potential publishers and narrow your target list to those who appear to deal in your kind of books.
- Demonstrate you can follow directions and will be easy to work with by customizing the format for your submissions to meet the exact specifications set by the publisher.
- Use the tools you have already developed, such as your preliminary research, to position yourself and your product to their greatest advantages. In other words, put your best feet forward.
- Add some lagniappe—something "extra" to leverage the chances your book will sell. An introduction by a famous person is one "extra." Another would be quotes from readers praising the manuscript.
- Make your cover letter sing. And count. Face it, if the screen-

ers don't like what they read in the cover letter, what are the chances they will even look at the sample from the manuscript? Zero. *Nada.* Count on it.

- Always, always remember: Publishers owe you nothing. What you owe them is a real opportunity to produce, together, a successful book. One that will make money for them, first. And for you, too, of course.
- Maintain, steadfastly and confidently, that you and your book will be good for their business. Tell them why. Succinctly and objectively. Show them how, with examples.

Chapter 5

Six Sure Things You Can Do
To Piss Off Your Publisher.
And End Up Sucking Hind Teat.

Before you get all in a twit over the language in the title of this chapter, remember we're talking about what sells. Whether you or Billy Graham like it or not, language of the street, used judiciously and in proper context, sells.

And why is that? Because it's real.

I am not advocating the irresponsible use of four-letter words. What I am saying is that their use to enhance the reality of meaning or dialogue is appropriate. If not overdone.

For those of you not from the South, the term "sucking hind teat" refers to the left-out position of the runt piglet whose number is one too many for ol' mom's spigots. The one that gets left behind when it's dinnertime.

Now that we've cleared up that little mystery, if you're willing to forgive me a bit of Tennessee Williams in the title, or maybe John Steinbeck, then let's move on to the real subject at hand.

To wit: It's a good idea to learn what it takes to keep in the good graces of your publisher. Why? Because, at any given time, that publisher has more books to produce than staff or resources to get the job done. Doesn't matter if it's Dime Box Jiffy Press or Simon & Schuster. They're overloaded. Have to be to make any money.

Sure, everybody's work gets done eventually. But whose work goes to the top of the stack? You guessed it. The authors whom the publisher's staff like and enjoy working with the most.

That's not only human nature. It's reality in the competitive business world.

Trouble is, though, publishers and authors alike tell me that many authors do things, innocently and without malice, that tend to address the first part of this chapter's title—the pissing-off part.

Do something once, and you'll probably be forgiven as just "naive." Do it twice, and you're sucking hind teat. For at least a couple of weeks. Keep on doing it, and you're dead meat. Road kill. Your work will get done, probably without any real concern or passion, about three days after the last minute. Like the governor calling the warden at 3:00 A.M. after the executioner threw the switch at midnight.

Oops!

Since I have a multitude of personal experience in this subject matter, having subjected my publisher's staff to almost every imaginable faux pas before I learned better—and because publishers tell me it would be ever so much easier and more pleasant for all concerned if authors just "knew better"—I have resolved to address this not-so-delicate subject. Straight out. Pulling no punches.

So here we go. We'll stick to six transgressions considered most flagrant, although I'm told some authors have come up with dozens of creative ways to make themselves somewhat despised around the old publishing house. And we won't worry about the order of significance. They're all bad things to do. This is not Letterman's Top-Ten countdown.

Transgression:
Pretend you know everything when, in fact, you're a neophyte.

This is a commonly displayed writer's trait that works for about fifteen minutes. Tops.

Bright people, and particularly bright and creative people, are curious. They want to know everything. And they don't want anybody to know that they really don't know anything about a given subject. After all, if you're qualified for Mensa, you ought to be able to skate through any conversation/discussion and pick up on enough to appear knowledgeable. Right?

Gong! Wrong.

When you try to act as if you know things about publishing you really don't, watch for the eyeballs of others in the room to simultaneously roll upward in their sockets until you're staring at a bunch of white eyes. Then you'll know you're busted.

Why put yourself and others through this embarrassment of synchronized eyeball action? Just admit, right up front, that you don't have a clue what the designer or editor is talking about. Stop them. Interrupt, politely, of course. Ask questions. Learn. And tell them, right out loud and with no apologies, that you're still learning and will probably be confused from time to time.

Know what will happen? They'll take extra pains with you to be sure you're with them. You will be appreciated. Instead of embarrassed. And disliked.

Transgression:
Become demanding. Insist that they do their jobs right. For you.

After all, if it weren't for you and your manuscript, they wouldn't even have jobs. So they ought to be ever grateful to you for all the opportunities you've provided for them. Right?

Shape them up. Yell at them a couple of times a week. Accuse them of being lazy and stupid and uninterested in you and your book. That ought to do it. Shouldn't it?

You bet. That'll do it, all right. It'll get you chunked to the bottom of both the work and give-a-damn stacks. If not handed your precious manuscript and shown to the exit. Permanently.

Don't do it. It's not only stupid, it's wrong and wrong-headed.

Remember, you are a guest on their premises. Behave like a guest. Writers who act like demanding jerks are never forgotten or forgiven. If a choice is to be made between spending time and money on one of two books, guess who gets the blue M&M? The author the publisher's staff likes.

And the jerk gets hind teat.

Transgression:
Expect unreasonable attention.

Sure, you're in a hurry. Why shouldn't you be? After all, you've got a little money and a lot of time invested in your manuscript. Tons of effort. A truckload of thinking. A lot of love, too. Blood. Sweat. Tears.

You want a book. And you want it yesterday.

Well, I have news for you. So do all the other authors in the house. And you know whose work is going to get a priority? Every time?

Not yours. Not if you continually question and push and badger the folks who are doing their best to make you a hero. As a matter of fact, the harder you push, the more you demand, the longer it's going to take. I guarantee it. Bet the farm on it. It's axiomatic.

Remember this: Whether you're building a house, painting a bus, or going from New York to Cairo, you can have any two of the following variables: speed, quality, economy. Any two. But never all three.

If you want your book in a hurry and you want it to be a quality product, you'd better be ready to fork over some serious overtime cash. Because you just sacrificed economy. If you want it economically and fast, forget about quality. If you want a quality product, produced economically . . . well, that takes time.

It's a good idea to discuss timetables and schedules, up front and dispassionately, with your publisher. They'll give you their best estimate as to when they think your book will be ready to release. Then add about six weeks to that estimate. They want you to be happy, so they will invariably mentally shave some time off the schedule.

Count on it taking a minimum of six months. Or go to a printer and pay to have it printed and bound in two weeks. Those are about the only two choices. And with the second, you get no designer, no editor, no marketing assistance, no sales assistance. You're totally on your own. But, by gum, it'll be fast.

Transgression:
Don't tell your publisher what you're doing.

This transgression almost always falls into the category of an oversight rather than a deliberate slight. Some authors just don't think to let their publishers know about things like events they have committed to attend, book signings, publicity efforts they have initiated. When you forget to inform your publisher, and particularly their sales staff, about the activities you're engaging in, you put them in a position of being embarrassed—even looking foolish and incompetent in their industry, the book trade.

Let's look at an example. Your publisher's sales department is working to accomplish several things for you simultaneous with the release of *Devil's Lust in the Dust Devils.* They call up the area marketing manager for XYZ Book Chain and suggest there is a relevant tie-in that merits an introductory store signing in Dust Devil, Arizona. To their surprise, they find that you have already arranged for that signing, have given an interview to the *Dust Devil Spin,* and will be appearing twice on a morning radio talk show, "Devils Today."

Good for you for having done all that preparation work for yourself. But would it not have been a good idea to let the publisher's sales department know what you were up to?

Your negligence in not keeping them informed has just wasted two days of phone-tag time. And embarrassed them in front of one of their biggest customers. And yours, too.

Result? At least one area marketing manager wonders if the two of you have your act together. No, the AMM *knows* the two of you don't. And that's a red flag.

"But," you protest, "it's just one AMM in one tiny market. Not a lot of sales potential there anyway. No harm done."

Wrong again.

That particular area marketing manager has responsibility for Phoenix, Tucson, Flagstaff, and Albuquerque. And if you think that area marketing managers and community relations managers in bookstore chains don't share information, you are wrong. One more time.

Your simple oversight, your lack of common business manners, has created a much bigger potential problem than you might ever imagine. And most of it accrues to you, in two ways. First, you are now a bit suspect when it comes to reliability within a major bookseller's organization. And, just as important, you have pissed off your publisher.

Oops.

Before I leave this subject, let me quickly add that keeping each other informed is obviously a two-way street. Your publisher needs to keep you informed as well. But they already know that. About the only reason they would deliberately fail to follow through is if . . . guess what? You've severely pissed them off.

Transgression:
Try to run their business.

This transgression covers a multitude of potential sins you can commit—out of ignorance, indifference, or lack of thought.

Let's keep it simple, because we're going to be looking into some more detail in specific areas a little later in this book. In Part III, in particular, we'll take a closer look at working with the various functional departments and individuals within the publisher's organization.

Meantime, please remember this humbling thought: Anybody can sit down and write a manuscript. Sure, it may be awful. Or worse than awful. But you, as an author, cannot (under any circumstances) edit your own manuscript. And, unless you are unusually multi-talented, you are not equipped to design a book. Particularly your own book.

Point? Your publisher employs specialists to edit, design, and help you market your book. They almost always know what they are doing. Just let them do their jobs. Without trying to micromanage everything they do.

They'll love you for giving them that respect. And remember what happens to authors and their manuscripts when the folks at the publishing company love them?

Right.

Transgression:
Try to monopolize their time.

We want the publishing staff to love you. But they don't want or need you to move in with them. Respect their time. And the fact that they are working with multiple authors on multiple manuscripts. They're doing a lot of things that don't involve you or the need for your presence.

Practice good business manners. It's that simple.

Communicate via e-mail whenever possible. Electronic mail is a nonintrusive medium. They can look at it and respond when they have time. You're not interrupting anything.

When you need to meet with them, ask for an appointment. Again, e-mail is a good way to let them know that you need to come by their offices. Be specific about why you need to see them, so they can be prepared. Give them an option of times: Thursday late in the day, Friday midmorning, or Friday afternoon? Let them decide. There are a dozen of them working for you. And there's only one of you. It's easier for you to accommodate their schedules than vice versa.

Restrain Your Creativity

Clearly, you can quite easily find many more ways to be offensive while dealing with your publisher. Creativity is a wonderful curse. No?

Just remember the one thing I've tried to stress in this chapter: Do whatever you can, naturally and without false fabrication, to stay on the good side of the publishing staff.

It all boils down to respect. You respect them, and they'll respect you. And when they respect you, who gets the best of the best they have to offer?

Numero Uno. Congratulations.

Devil's Lust in the Dust Devils? *Ha!*
We'll show that jerk what a real dust devil's like!

Part III

And the Manuscript Begat Words (and More Words).

Right Up Front:
Who Does What to Whom?
And When? Exactly.

You have completed a stack of submissions. For each one of them, you have followed directions perfectly. You have formatted and re-arranged and included some of the "smarts" you gathered from your research panel. You have honed the cover letters until they fairly sing.

And you've started sending them in. You know that some have already arrived, because you've enclosed self-addressed, stamped post-cards for the publishers to notify you that your package has been received. And you've gotten a couple of them back. Postcards, that is.

You've even started to follow up.

The phone rings.

It's Earthy Publications, LLP, and they want to speak to the au-thor of *Devil's Lust in the Dust Devils*. In fact, they want to speak to you in person. "Can you come in to our offices next Tuesday morning at 9:30?" Hosanna! A real publisher wants to talk to you about your manuscript. Maybe even publish it!

Suddenly, reality sets in. What if they offer you a contract? You don't know anything about contracts. Do you? Probably not. Is it okay to ask them to take it with you and review it? Maybe even have a lawyer look it over? Or would that be rude? Would they just decide not to fool with you and your book if you're not willing to sign on the spot?

The phone call and meeting you've been working toward for months—your greatest dreams—have now become a potentially scary, daunting possibility.

What if they tell you they're only interested if you can cut twenty percent of the length? There's not a word of fat in your manuscript, you've convinced yourself. Suppose they want it to be 150,000 words? Where could you come up with another 25,000? There is nothing more to say. Padding would ruin the story, wouldn't it? What can you do to get ready? Is it too late to get some advice from a lawyer? What a catharsis!

No need for panic. In the next few pages, we're going to talk about these questions and get you ready. So you can go into your long-awaited meeting at-ease. And comfortable. Even semi-prepared.

Instead of lapsing into Whatifsville, have a glass of wine. Instead of worrying about what might or might not happen, think about how good you're going to be when you finally get the chance to sell your own book. And how many of those little gems you're going to sell. Picture *Devil's Lust in the Dust Devils* on the *New York Times* Best-Seller List. For sixty-eight consecutive weeks.

In short, enjoy yourself now, while you may. Because, believe it or not, your work is just beginning.

And, oh, yes. Take a few minutes to read on to see what you need to know to be ready for that meeting. Next Tuesday morning at 9:30.

At this point, you may be a bit skeptical. After all, most good publishers won't try to take advantage of you. Will they? Especially Earthy Publications, LLP. They have a good reputation. Don't they? Except among church ladies maybe?

Why not just grab that contract (you know they're going to hand you one), sign that puppy, and get on with becoming famous? Chances are pretty good that doing just that wouldn't get you into any real trouble. At least not at first. But later, you'll be in for some real surprises if you don't take the time to understand the contract. Thoroughly. And up front. *Before* you sign it.

Why is this so important? What is the big deal about understanding the ins-and-outs of what you're about to sign? And live with for years, possibly?

Here are some very important reasons you must understand the contract:

- *To avoid distracting surprises down the road.* Once you get the sales juggernaut cranked up, you do not need to find yourself disagreeing with your publisher about clauses you didn't bother to understand to begin with. You need to be able to focus on what? On selling. Good thinking.
- *To practice what I've been telling you about the importance of a good relationship with your publisher.* Contractual disagreements up front are healthy. If they are necessary, get them out of the way. Now. *Ex post facto* disagreements are just symptoms of sloppiness on the part of the author. And they're guaranteed to strain a business relationship that should, and can, be pleasant all the way around. As a matter of fact, if you are going to be successful and maximize your chances to market your book intelligently, your relationship with your publisher just has to be pleasant. And it's up to you to try your best to do your part. Right from the get-go.
- Your publisher, whichever company it may be, is running a business. *Once you have signed your contract, the publisher bases its decisions on dealing with you and your book on the terms of that contract.* If you get into a battle royal with them somewhere down the line, they won't know how to deal with you. And they will quickly lose enthusiasm for the whole idea of dealing with you.

Period.

Have I convinced you? Good.

Let's take a look, now, at some of the more important aspects of publisher contracts—those things you will want to pay particular attention to. One caveat: I am not an attorney. I do not dispense legal advice. What follows is not to be construed as legal advice. Just common business sense.

Fair enough?

For this first list, let's assume the publisher is buying your manuscript; i.e., that you are not self-publishing:

- On exactly what basis are you being paid? Advance? Commission? Royalty on sales, based on volume? Be sure

Chapter 6: Right Up Front: Who Does What to Whom? And When? Exactly.

43

you understand how the amount of money you will eventually receive is going to be calculated. Your publisher's business office will be glad to explain it to you. Don't sign until you get an explanation, repeat it aloud to the publisher's representative, and receive an affirmative that you do, in fact, understand how your receipts will be calculated. This need not, and should not, be an unpleasant meeting. Just stick with it until you know, for sure, the details.

- What will the publisher provide as its part of the agreement? An editor? A book design? A dust cover design? Marketing assistance? Exactly what kind of marketing assistance? What kind of promotional materials come with the deal? Who will pay for them?
- What, exactly, does the contract say you will bring to the agreement? Precisely what is expected of you? When? Now is the time to be sure you know what you are committing to do. After you sign, you're committed. End of discussion.

Those are the important things, in my nonlegal opinion. That's it. Not complicated. Not difficult.

Should you have an attorney look over the contract before you sign it? Would that be okay with the publisher? Will asking them for a copy to take with you to review and return with questions pose any threat to your future working relationship?

It is never a bad idea to have an attorney check out a contract. Two things to remember, though: First, almost every publisher's contract is ninety-nine percent boilerplate with a few blanks to fill in. They print them up in pads, tear off a set, and fill in the blanks for you. Or they have them on a diskette in their computer and fill in the blanks. Point is, what's in the blanks is really what counts most. It hardly seems worth having an attorney read five pages of boilerplate and suggest changes to that. Concentrate on the fill-ins.

Second, not every attorney is familiar with or competent in every phase of contract law. If you decide to employ an attorney, even for a quick review, find one who specializes in intellectual property law. He or she will not waste time on dissecting the boilerplate. They'll go right to the blanks and see what the fill-ins say.

As far as the publisher's attitude toward asking to take the contract to look it over and come back with questions—not to worry. Publishing is a business. You, as an author, are about to enter into a business relationship. Of course, it's not only acceptable but also smart to read what you're being asked to sign and be sure you understand it. The publisher will welcome your interest and be glad to answer your questions. Why? Because they don't want any surprises down the road either.

What if you are self-publishing? In that case, you will want to understand the economics of the book business, too. How many copies will you be printing? What will that quantity cost you? On a per unit basis, would it cost you significantly less to increase the size of the order? All these are fair questions that you must understand the answers to, whether you're paying to have your book printed or being paid a royalty based on sales.

Remember one thing, and you'll be okay. Inform yourself in a businesslike fashion before you sign. Understand what you're signing and what it means to both parties—what you and the publisher are promising each other. That's it.

Exhibit C. Book Economics–Example

Devil's Lust in the Dust Devils
(125,000 Words, 450 Pages, 6 by 9, Hardback)

	Per Unit Sold at Retail
Retail Selling Price	$30.00
Discount to Distributor (50%)	15.00
Publisher's Net Cash Receipts	15.00
Author's Royalty of Net Cash Receipts (10%)	1.50
Cost of Goods (Manufacturing Costs-Fully Loaded)	7.50
Shipping Costs	1.00
Promotional Costs Allocated	1.50
Publisher's Gross Profit	3.50
Publisher's Overhead	1.50
Publisher's Net Profit	$2.00

This is just a rough example and assumes your contract calls for a royalty of ten percent of the net cash receipts to the publisher. Sure, the publisher is

Chapter 6: Right Up Front: Who Does What to Whom? And When? Exactly.

45

making more money than you are, because they have put up the money and are taking all the risk. You can make all the money if you want to finance the project and take the risk. I do not advise that approach unless you have a lot of business experience, and know the book trade—cold. Be sure your contract does not call only for a flat percentage of the net cash receipts. The more books you sell, the higher the percentage of the net cash receipts you should receive (e.g., 10% the first 5,000 copies, 12% the second 5,000 copies, 14% after 10,000 copies).

Chapter 7

Love Your Editor.
More Than Yourself.

Pay attention to the title of this chapter. It contains a deep and important message for all authors.

A good editor will improve your manuscript. Immeasurably.

A good editor will make you look smart and talented. Smarter and more talented than you really are. Really.

A good editor will help you sell more books. And make more money. For you and the publisher. Hallelujah!

A good editor deserves your respect. And, if you're not respectful? If you're not pleasant to work with? Guess what? A good editor can "overlook" the holes in your manuscript, which may make you look foolish and untalented. And ensure you make as little money as possible.

So, love your editor. More than yourself.

What's implicit in those two statements, the title of this chapter?

Just this: There will be times when you will need to swallow your ego, your pride of authorship, your ownership of words, phrases, and clauses—dependent and independent—and open up your mind to the very likely possibility that your editor's ideas and suggestions are better than what's already in your manuscript.

This is going to happen. Count on it. And be ready to give your editor the benefit of your biased doubt. Yes, it is, too. Biased, that is.

And why is that important? Two reasons: First, remember, you want and need to be respectful to remain in the good graces of the entire staff at your publisher's business. That includes the editor. After all, they already like your manuscript to some degree, or you'd never get to meet an editor. Or anybody else, for that matter.

Second, and even more important—*it's your editor's responsibility to improve your manuscript.* Let's look a little further into that idea.

And let's start at the beginning, with the most basic question: *"Why do I need an editor anyway?* After all, I have edited the manuscript. Several times. I have had a reader panel of twenty-eight people give me useful, even helpful input. I absolutely know what I have in the manuscript. I think it's ready."

Wrong!

Think about it. An author is probably the single person worst suited to edit his or her own manuscript. From just a mechanical point of view, the author knows what was intended to be in every chapter, paragraph, and sentence. Knows what word is supposed to be where. And so, the brain "sees" what was intended, instead of seeing reality. The eyes don't readily see typos, mistakes, syntax errors, factual discrepancies, continuity lapses because the creator of the whole entity sees and reads what was intended. Which is not necessarily what resulted.

That means somebody needs to at least proofread, at the very minimum.

Now, a few authors I have questioned on this subject actually think of an editor as a proofreader. Editors may also be proofreaders. But a good proofreader is seldom an editor. They're different animals. With different talents.

Before we get bogged down in compound-complex sentences with multiple dependent clauses, let's just cut to the chase.

What is an editor? And what is the editor's role?

Following is a list of many of the disciplines a good editor will bring to a manuscript. This isn't necessarily an exhaustive list. Feel free to add to it. But don't overlook or discount any of the things on it. They're all important.

Style monitor. Your editor will be intimately familiar with publisher's style. How to handle numbers, where to place commas, when to use italics. Writers often grow up as trained journalists, in which case they become used to and intimately familiar with the stylebook of the Associated Press. It's the standard for most news organizations worldwide. But the AP style differs significantly from the *Chicago Manual of Style* used by most publishers. So the first job of an editor is to create style consistency. And accuracy.

Why should a writer care about this part of the job? Probably ought not to worry much about it, except to learn such things as numbers up to ninety-nine are usually spelled out. And hyphenated. Just for future reference. And to demonstrate that you're learning.

Continuity monitor. Every manuscript of any length will contain threads of recurring concepts, characters, events that are referred to, time and again, in the text. Any lapse of continuity will confuse the mental picture the reader will have formed and cause that reader a perplexing disconnect.

For example, in the first chapter of *Devil's Lust in the Dust Devils,* you have described the beautiful and irresistible Clarabelle's home as "an imposing, three-story Georgian mansion, complete with thirty-foot-tall pillars in front of a wide, plank porch across the entire face of the mansion." Then, in Chapter 7, as Black Bart rides his big sorrel stallion up the winding drive, arriving at Clarabelle's estate for the first time, he sees "a stately manse in the ante-bellum style, with a porch large enough for a rousing game of croquet."

"What's wrong with that?" you ask. Just a bit of linguistic variety so as not to become boring with descriptions. But a good editor will quickly spot that a "Georgian" mansion and an "ante-bellum" manse are not necessarily of the same architectural styles. And the editor will know that the mind-picture the reader likely formed (at the first description in Chapter 1) will conflict in the reader's mind's eye with the second description in Chapter 7. And that editor will tell you to pick one or the other, but stick to the same description every time you describe the house.

This is just one simple example. In any manuscript, there are dozens of opportunities for continuity lapses, or disconnects. A good

Chapter 7: Love Your Editor. More Than Yourself.

49

editor will catch, and repair, all of them. Result? Consistency that does not confuse the reader.

Clarity monitor. A good editor will catch and fix lapses in the language of the manuscript that seem to be confusing, or—at least—not crystal clear the first time through. Every manuscript, no matter how hard you have worked on it, will contain a few of these obscurities. Think of the editor as an obscurity scrubber.

"How about an example of this?" you ask.

Okay. Your book, *Devil's Lust in the Dust Devils,* is set in the 1890s. References to locomotives should include the adjective "steam." Use of words or phrases not yet in existence in the 1890s will cause yet more disconnects. Words like "plastic." Or "atomic." Or colloquialisms such as "Yo mama." Admittedly, these are extreme examples, but you might be amazed at how much of the current lexicon has a way of slipping into text set 125 years ago.

Your editor will catch these little gems and fix them.

Grammar and punctuation monitor. Think of your editor as "Miss Thistlebottom," the stodgy, old grammarian seventh-grade English teacher who terrorized you with her red pen. You remember her, don't you? Gray hair pulled tightly into a bun behind her head. Pince-nez glasses perched on the bridge of her nose. Red grading pen tucked behind her left ear, a position from which she could "quick-draw" to lower your grade one letter for every grammatical error.

Only now, as opposed to the seventh-grade English class, you're delighted for the markdown. Makes you look smarter this time. Instead of dumber. Hosanna!

Concept monitor. No matter how well it may be crafted, there are always twists and turns, a little added irony, a small directional change that will improve a story. Make it more believable. More interesting. Better reading. Give your editor the latitude to make these kinds of suggestions. And take them seriously. You don't necessarily have to buy every one of them, but consider them. Think about them. If you don't agree with them, see if you can, logically and rationally, dissuade the editor. If you can't do that, accept the suggestions. Gracefully—and gratefully.

You've just improved your book.

Eliminator of excess baggage. Overwriting is an occupational hazard that all writers face and must contend with. We love the words. Individually. In combinations, long and short. Verbosity is a natural tendency. A good editor will almost always shorten a manuscript, and greatly improve it in the process. Once again, we have to be careful not to become overenamored with our own text. If it's overwritten for the editor, you can bet it's also overwritten for the intended readers.

Reader ombudsman. A good editor will take on the mindset of the target reader of your book. Since *Devil's Lust in the Dust Devils,* as you learned from your research and, as subsequently confirmed by your editor's experience, appeals to women, twenty-five to forty-nine, and to men older than sixty-five, your editor will "pretend" to be among one of these groups as he or she reads your manuscript. That editor will adopt the mindset of the age and gender of the intended reader and, subsequently, catch important disconnects with that group.

Now that we've taken a closer look at what it is an editor brings to the party, let's look, very briefly, at the author's role in the process.

How do you approach working with an editor?

How do you get the most out of a good editor?

Other than a few gross generalizations, there are no pat answers to these questions. This is not meant to dodge the issue but rather to point out that each editor is an individual. And each individual editor has his or her preferred way of working, of approaching a manuscript and its author.

My strong suggestion is that you meet with your assigned editor, up front, ask how he or she wants to proceed, and listen. Take notes. Pay attention. If you let the editor proceed in the fashion in which he or she prefers to work, then you will be getting the best help you can get from that editor.

When you ask these questions and then listen, remember what's going to happen? You're demonstrating respect for that editor and the role of the editor in general. And who will the publisher's staff appreciate for that? Right! You. And who will get the best in terms of attention and resources? Right again. Numero Uno.

Just for the sake of argument, let's suppose you believe you have gone out of your way to listen, respect, work with, and cooperate with your editor. But it's just not working. You find the editor yelling at you, with fire in her eyes. And you find yourself wanting to yell back. But you are carefully restraining that urge because of what you have learned here. In short, the process is just falling apart. And you believe the manuscript is suffering. You know you are suffering.

Is it acceptable to ask the publisher for a different editor? How acceptable it is depends on the personalities involved. But it certainly is possible. And it may, in reality—although rarely—become necessary.

Before you stick your neck out too far, however, and risk wholesale alienation, be sure of the ground you're standing on. Have you truly bent over backward to be cooperative and helpful? Have you been open to listening and considering every suggestion your editor has made? Have you been measured and reasonable in your responses to the editor's suggestions?

In short, if you have put in 125 percent of your very best behavior, and it's just not working, go forward and ask. Humbly. And politely.

Please don't construe this as an invitation to play ping-pong with people just to find someone who will agree with you. If you are inclined to get second, third, and fourth opinions until you find someone who agrees with you, do not—I repeat, *do not*—ask for another editor. Under any circumstances. Ever. Because *you* are the problem, even though you'll keep asking others besides me until you find someone who will agree it's the editor who has the problem. Not you.

Not to beat the trite dead horse, but just remember two things from this chapter, if nothing else:

- You absolutely, positively must have a trained editor for your manuscript.
- That editor wants your manuscript to be as good as it can possibly be and therefore will work hard to achieve that level of perfection. Let it happen. To paraphrase Smokey (or is it Smoky?—see why you need an editor?) the Bear, "Only you can prevent a better manuscript." [Editor's note: It's Smokey, George. And no "the" before "Bear."]

Exhibit D. What a Good Editor Brings to the Editing Party.

A Checklist.
- Talents an author simply cannot apply to his or her own manuscript.
- Consistency in style.
- Consistency in continuity.
- Greater clarity.
- Improved grammar.
- Perfect punctuation.
- Improved concepts and a better story.
- Tight text that's not overwritten.
- A gut-check representation of the target audience.

Exhibit E. What a Good Author Brings to the Editing Party.

A Checklist.
- An understanding of the editor's role.
- An appreciation of and respect for the editor's talents.
- An open mind.
- Flexibility and willingness to listen. And to change.
- The good grace, and good sense, to work the way the editor likes to work.
- Unending gratitude for the improvements the editor will, invariably, make in the manuscript.

Chapter 7: Love Your Editor. More Than Yourself.

53

Is Your Artistic Ability Showing?
Or Is That Your Posterior, Maybe?

"I think I'm getting confused." Your book designer scratches her head, picks up her well-chewed, yellow, number-two Eagle Mirado wooden pencil, and sits back in her chair, looking at you quizzically.

"Nothing to be confused about," you respond. Pleasantly, of course, taking care not to be condescending. "I've tried to make it crystal clear."

"Okay. Let's review, then. You said your research indicates the book's main appeal is to women twenty-five to forty-nine. Right?"

"Right."

"And it also appeals to men over sixty-five. Right?"

"Absolutely. Now you're getting it." You smile, trying not to show your impatience with this tedious repetition—at least the fourth time in the last fifteen minutes you've been over the same ground.

"Because of these two completely different and mutually exclusive audiences, you think the book should be designed to look both frilly and rustic?" A pained look comes over the designer's face. As if just repeating your crystal-clear ideas has brought on a sudden and vicious attack of hemhorroidal discomfort. So to speak.

"That's exactly right, Amber. Feminine and rustic, I think I said." You grin at her, hoping to bridge the gap between her puzzled expression and the squirming in her chair. You notice she hasn't used her pencil yet. "I think you're on the right track now."

"I don't." She looks about ready to burst into tears.

"What's the problem?" you ask, innocently and unthinkingly. "Seems like you understand exactly what I want. But you're not happy about it. What's wrong?"

She looks nervously at you, a black cloud forming over her head, complete with rolling thunder and chain lightning. As if trying to decide whether to bolt from the room or club you with her chair. There seem to be no other immediate options on her mind. Finally, she takes a deep breath, leans right into your face like one of Seinfeld's "close-talkers," and lets her frustration out.

"What's wrong," she begins through clenched teeth, "is that either you're not thinking about what you're saying ... or you, sir, are incapable of thought. I have still to decide which." She sits back, regaining her nervous bolt-or-club-you aura.

Well, that's a fine thing. It's taken only fifteen minutes to get to the point you're ready to ask for someone else to design *Devil's Lust in the Dust Devils*. This woman obviously doesn't get it. And it's becoming pretty clear, pretty fast, that she considers you something of an idiot, besides.

You think to yourself, *I'll make one last-ditch effort to salvage this relationship.* So you sit back, signaling you're ready to give her some more space (and move yourself out of range of her chair should she actually opt to grab it and whack you with it).

"Amber, somehow I have upset you. This all seems so clear to me that I'm having some trouble here figuring out what's bothering you. If we're going to work closely together for the next month, I need to know what I've done to upset you." There. You have pitched the problem back at her. Obviously, she's the one who's not up to speed here.

Fast forward one week. You're out of the hospital, having at least partially recovered from having a swivel chair wrapped around your head. Your left arm is still in a sling, but the pain is almost gone.

All that time in the hospital gave you the chance to think about what happened to your relationship with the book designer. You ask every visitor who comes in to tell you what "look" they would want in a book that appeals to younger women and older men. Every one of them says essentially the same thing: "Well, you can't have both. If

Chapter 8: Is Your Artistic Ability Showing? Or Is That Your Posterior, Maybe?

55

your primary audience is younger women, better give it a look that will appeal to that group. Try to give it a dual look and you'll end up with tossed salad—a completely incomprehensible hodgepodge."

Well, duh!

You wonder, as you limp up the front steps of your publisher's offices, whether there is any chance Amber, a great young book designer, will be willing to give your book another try. Or will she hit you again?

To your complete surprise and total embarrassment, Amber is happy to see you. She has something to show you. Two comprehensive design concepts. One is clearly feminine. The other clearly rustic and masculine. Then she shows you yet a third option. Your option. A combination of the two on several spreads.

If your in-hospital poll, with unanimous (and obvious) results, was not proof enough, Amber has provided you with show-and-tell. Visual proof that your demonstration of artistic direction showed one thing above all others.

Your posterior.

Of course, this is a silly and exaggerated little scenario. Exaggerated to make a critically important point: *Let trained and talented people do their jobs.*

Remember that word "respect"? In your enthusiasm to demonstrate your "smarts" about the appeal of *Devil's Lust in the Dust Devils,* you went too far. And now you realize that even though you have a handle on who will be interested in and attracted to the book, that doesn't necessarily make you an art director. Or a book designer. Any more than it makes you an editor.

Just because the example is silly and exaggerated doesn't mean that a good book designer won't *want* to club you with a chair when you, totally unqualified as you are, try to tell her how to do her job.

Well, my now more thoughtful and less artistically talented friends, if we can learn how to get the best out of an editor, then *surely* we can also learn how to get the best from a book designer. Right?

Correct. So let's get to it.

I think we'll just skip right over the business of why you need a book designer—based on the lesson learned by being clubbed with a swivel chair—and move directly into the next phase of our discovery: What is the role of the book designer? What can the designer do to help you sell more copies of *Devil's Lust in the Dust Devils?*

Ordering the Eye. The primary job of the dust cover (or front cover, if it's a paperback) of your book is to draw attention to itself on the bookstore shelf. To stand out among the thousands of books it will be competing with and beckon the shopper, "Look at me! Pick me up! Thumb through my pages! Buy me!" Think of it as packaging. Or a point-of-sale display. Even the spine is an important design element. (By the way, bookstores will not stock a book whose spine does not contain the title, author's last name, and publisher identification. Self-publishers, pay attention.)

One job of the book designer is to make the exterior of the book inviting, attractive, different. In art direction, the process is called "ordering the eye." That is, causing the observers' eyes to see, comprehend, and understand what's important about *Devil's Lust in the Dust Devils.*

In short, to invite sampling. Or purchase.

Visual cohesion. Your book is a love story set in the 1890s. It needs to visually tell the potential buyer exactly that. Instantly. On the outside and on the inside. Your book designer will select typefaces, colors, design motifs, formats, shapes, even blank (or white) spaces that will say "end of the nineteenth century" in visual ways. Subtle, instant communication.

A good book designer knows how to do these things.

Content representation. Just as your book's "look" must be true to the era of the story it contains, so must the visual treatment, throughout the book, be relevant to and supportive of the story line. Chapter by chapter. Page by page. Paragraph by paragraph. Will you choose to use old, faded photographs? Or illustrations? What kind of illustrations? Line drawings? Halftones? Continuous tones? Even the leading of the type (the space between the lines) can convey a feel, an attitude. All these decisions will lead to a blend of visual treatments that will either enhance, or distract from, the content of your book. Unless you are an incredibly talented communicator who both writes and art directs well, and unless you have already designed several books, my advice is to let the book designer do his or her job.

And be grateful they know how to do, well, what you don't have a clue how to do.

Chapter 8: Is Your Artistic Ability Showing? Or Is That Your Posterior, Maybe?

57

A total visual package. Just as a box of Kellogg's Corn Flakes shows you, visually and instantly, what's inside that box, so must a book's design communicate instantly. Just as that same corn flakes box gives you detailed information in the form of nutritional analyses, product chemistry, and why you should buy and consume its contents, so must a book's packaging.

But corn flakes boxes only have to have exterior designs. Each flake doesn't have to be designed to be visually appealing and convey a look, feel, and taste level.

Not so with a book.

Think of each page of a book as one corn flake in a fifteen-ounce package—an individual flake that has to be custom designed to be appealing. Now you have an idea of what the job of the book designer entails. Not a job for amateurs, for sure.

Good design takes time. If it is going to "fit" your book, the designer must have time to do his or her work. And that includes discussions with the editor about the book's subject, its tone and style—all the things you think make *Devil's Lust in the Dust Devils* the unique product you want it to be.

Then, like a fine wardrobe, "clothing" must be designed, cut, stitched, and finished in a coordinated fashion to dress up your book. Appropriate accents will then be added to enhance the total "look."

Every element is custom made for your individual product. Every decision is made with an eye toward helping you sell the most books possible.

So, what should the author's role be with the book designer?

Input provider. Answer all the questions your designer may have after he or she has had a chance to go through your manuscript, talk with the editor, and become familiar with your story. Volunteer only information that is pertinent to the question being asked. A designer is visualizing—seeing alternatives in his or her mind's eye. So a random bit of information thrown in, gratuitously, will only interrupt that series of visions, and waste time. Stick to the subject.

Sounding board. Clearly, decisions as to which of the alternative visual treatments works best will have to be made. Your book designer wants your input. He or she will ask you what you think, listen to what you have to say. And then do the right thing—even if it's not your first choice. Give the designer that freedom. They know what they're doing. You only have vague notions of the whole process.

Gatherer and collector. There may be times when your designer will have a great idea for a photo or illustration or visual element—something that obviously will enhance the appeal of the book, but which is not readily at hand. Go find it. Secure a copy and written permission, for the files, to reprint that copy. In short, do the mundane legwork so your designer can design. Look at it this way: Either of you can do the legwork, but you can't design. Isn't it more efficient to let the designer design while you do the legwork? Of course it is. Be a good and quick helper. You'll be loved for it.

And remember what you get when you're loved?

Right!

Cheerleader. You know how good it makes you feel when someone you respect says something complimentary about your writing? Makes you want to do even better, right? Art directors are no different. When you see something in the design that you really like, say so. On the spot. It will not only make the designer feel good and want to do better but also lets the designer know that he or she is on the right track. At least as far as you are concerned. And, as long as you continue to respect them and their role, they will want to please you. To end up with a product you're proud of.

Why? Because you'll sell more of them than if you're unhappy. And everybody will make more money.

Not complicated. Just like I promised.

About now, we ought to do a quick review. We've figured out how to get into and stay in the good graces of the publisher. We now understand our roles with the editor and book designer and—very importantly—how to get the most attention and best work from them.

In all of these things, there's not much for the author to do besides respect everyone else's roles and be supportive. So, when do you get to spring back into high gear? About the time your designer has nailed down the "feel," it's time for you to crank up your marketing planning machine.

Chapter 8: Is Your Artistic Ability Showing? Or Is That Your Posterior, Maybe?

59

Say what?

Your marketing planning machine.

Don't worry. You're not supposed to know much about that yet. But in the next three chapters, we'll see how to plan to be a marketing success, and how to work that plan to ensure success.

Take a break. Rest a little. You're about to get very, very busy.

"Watch out for small potholes when you're on the road that leads to a great book design."

Part IV

And the Words Became a Book. Hallelujah!

Chapter 9

Plan to Succeed.
Or You'll Surely Fail.

We started off this whole subject by pointing out that, with more than six billion people on the earth these days, you will surely be able to find enough of them who will be interested in the subject of your book to sell a boatload of copies. Once your book designer begins the several-weeks-long process of designing your book, it's time for you to crank up the search for these buyers.

Where do you look for them? Where are they hiding? How do you find them? How do you get your message to them? What do you have to do to sell them a book?

Not to worry. As promised, the process is not complicated or difficult. Certainly not as tough as creating a book from scratch.

The answers to all these, and many more, questions can be found by taking a stroll down marketing lane. Along the way, I will show you how to construct a *bona fide* marketing plan that will help you circle the wagons around those younger women and older men most predisposed to being interested in *Devil's Lust in the Dust Devils*. Together, we'll discover how to plan to be successful selling the book. And how to work the plan to ensure that you'll be successful.

Here we go.

There are usually five major sections to a real marketing plan:

- The objective(s).
- The strategies.
- The tactics.
- The timetable.
- The budget.

They have to be approached in this order (to avoid chaos), just as a house is built starting with the foundation, then the walls, the roof, the exterior and interior finishing. Developing a marketing plan is, in fact, a building-block process. Each step forms the foundation for, and leads directly and logically to, the next step.

In fairness to product marketing managers out there who develop 400-page annual and long-term marketing plans for their products, I should tell you there are many other parts to a marketing plan than the five listed above. But they are not critical to the structural integrity of the plan or to its success in the marketplace. They simply identify the situation. Give the background. Report on the competition and its strategies and pricing. Recapitulate research results. And, in general, provide information for anyone not familiar with the product, its channels of distribution, its pricing—those kinds of things. So they can read the plan, cold, and understand the relevance of the objectives, strategies, tactics, schedules/timetables, and the rationale and economics behind the budget.

You certainly are free to include all these parts in your plan, if you wish. In the interest of getting right to the heart of what will make or break your sales success, we'll be concentrating on what I call "the big five." A complete outline of a prototype marketing plan is included at the end of this chapter. The big five are in boldface type.

We'll begin by summarizing the other elements in this abbreviated listing:

Product: A Hardback Book
Product Name: *Devil's Lust in the Dust Devils*
Brief Product Description: 6 x 9 inches; approximately 450 pages;
    125,000 words; illustrated
Retail Selling Price: $27.95

Release Date: Spring 2004
Publisher: Earthy Publications, LLP
Author: (Your Name Goes Here)
Primary Target: Women, twenty-five to forty-nine
Secondary Target: Men older than sixty-five

With that information "in the can," so to speak, we can get right on with addressing the "big five" of your marketing plan. As we learned earlier, we'll start with:

The Objective(s)

This will be the shortest section of your plan. The statement of your objective(s) will occupy less than half a page. Much less. Double-spaced, of course.

What is an objective? It is a simple statement with two parts: What you want to have happened at the end of a specified period of time (usually a year); and how you are going to measure, or quantify, whether you have succeeded in reaching that objective. Sometimes there is more than one objective—a *primary* objective and a *secondary* objective. If you have more than that to say, either you're working way too hard at the process or you haven't quite figured out how to state an objective. Yet.

That's it. What could be easier?

Let's try out an objective:

"*To sell a minimum of 2,500 copies of* Devil's Lust in the Dust Devils *within one year of initial release of the first edition.*"

There you have it. That's all there is to it. You have, in only twenty-four words (six of them the title of your book) satisfied the definition of an objective. You have said what you want to have happen, by when. And you have established a quantifiable measuring device (2,500 copies) by which to determine if you have met your objective at the end of the time period (one year from release).

"Well," you're saying, "that's not a very lofty objective. What if I want my book to become a million seller?"

That's fine. Go for it. Just be sure the strategies, tactics, timetable, and budget that follow will really support such a mega-target. Remember, at the end of the year, you are going to have to give your-

Chapter 9: Plan to Succeed. Or You'll Surely Fail.

65

self a grade. Did I make my objective? If your budget will stand an expenditure of $10 million or so, you might have a fighting chance to sell a whole lot more than 2,500 copies.

I chose that number because it is a reasonable and achievable number for a first-time author's first book—provided that author is prepared to devote a lot of evenings and weekends making it happen. And that same author won't have to mortgage the farm to support the effort's budget.

Set your objective with your total time and monetary resources in mind. My number (2,500) is an achievable number for an author who can devote part-time to the sales process and can't afford to spend more than he or she will ever make in royalties to achieve it.

Strategies

Strategies are a bit more detailed than objectives. They describe what actions you are going to take, in general terms, to achieve the objective. Taken together, they answer the question: "How am I going to meet my objective?"

Strategies most often are organized, or grouped, by like activities. Rather than try to explain what that means (and get into some convoluted verbal tête-à-tête that will cause the whole magilla to seem complicated), let's just develop some strategies.

You'll get the picture. Immediately.

Here we go.

Promotional Strategies

- Develop brand identities for your book and for yourself. Here's how: Based on what your reader panel has told you, answer these questions about your product: Who most likely wants to read this kind of book? Why do you think these groups might want to read it? What two or three major attributes of the book will give them the most compelling reasons to buy it?

    The answers to these questions will define your book's brand. Write it down: "Women twenty-five to forty-nine and men older than sixty-five will want to read my book because it is the kind of historical love story that provides both groups vicarious experiences they will never encounter in the real world." As far as branding yourself, that is even easier. Just ask yourself who would be an expert chronicler of the Old West in the 1890s. Likely it will be someone akin to a member of the cast of *Little House on the Prairie.* Then become that person. Dress for the part. Practice in front of a mirror. Or in front of a sympathetic group. It's easier than you think. Don't freak. We'll talk more about this later.

- Develop a comprehensive press kit containing a book synopsis, a general news release about the book, a short feature story related to the content of the book, a brief biography of the author, a photo of the author, and a signed sample book. Distribute individual copies, as appropriate.

- Develop and employ promotional materials, including a preproduction announcement mailer, point-of-sale posters (including multiple seasonal variations), postcard invitations to appearances and signings.

- Develop mailing lists, among the primary markets that will be included in the first year's activities, of book and entertainment editors of print media and producers of electronic (radio and TV) talk shows that regularly include authors as guests.

Sales Strategies

- Develop a detailed schedule of events and bookstore signings, with unit sales projections for each. Update frequently. And keep your publisher's sales department informed.

- Call on store managers and owners of independent bookstores in the initial markets included in the introductory effort. Introduce your "brand," provide sample copies, and schedule signings and appearances. Keep your publisher's sales department informed.

- Call on store managers and area marketing managers (or community relations managers) of chain store booksellers in initial introductory markets. Introduce your "brand," provide sample copies, and schedule signings and appearances. Keep your publisher's sales department informed.

Chapter 9: Plan to Succeed. Or You'll Surely Fail.

67

- Offer programs to civic clubs, book clubs, friends of library associations, and other groups in initial introductory markets. Schedule signings and appearances. Keep your publisher's sales department informed.
- Develop a signings/appearance kit, containing all the materials you will need for a signing, and have it ready to go with you at a moment's notice.
- Develop a database list of bookstore contacts—store managers, area marketing managers, community relations managers, and regional managers. Update and expand it regularly.

That's enough to give you an idea of how to list strategies. Take care not to make your strategy list so formidable that you have no hope of accomplishing all of it. Keep it simple and manageable. Remember this: It is better to do a few things in a small area *very well* than to do a little bit of a lot of things superficially. And scattered all over the map.

Those strategies listed above are certainly doable on a part-time basis. All that will be required is discipline. But that's true of any activity at which you really want to succeed. Right?

Remember Nike. Just do it.

Your publisher's sales department will certainly help you with the production of materials. They have the graphics on their computers already. You don't have to invent all this stuff on your own. Sit down with them and divide up responsibilities. One more hint: They will also be helpful in setting up signings and event appearances, as well as in helping you find sources for your lists.

Tactics

Tactics are like a recipe. They are a step-by-step listing of exactly what you are going to do to accomplish each strategy. So, there may be multiple tactics for each strategy, just as there are multiple strategies for each objective.

Since this is not brain surgery, I will illustrate tactics more in-depth in the next chapter. Right now, just for practice, why not take one each of your promotional and sales strategies and see if you can develop the tactics that answer the question "What, exactly, am I going to do to achieve this strategy?"

Timetable

The timetable is just that—a chronological listing of your tactics. Take your list of tactics and put them on a calendar, one you can carry around with you, whether it's a hard copy or on a diskette in your laptop computer. The most useful form, I think, for busy people is a weekly timetable. It's nothing more than a list of things (tactics) to be done that week.

Again, the key is discipline. Making sure you get everything on your list of tactics done. When it is supposed to be done.

Budget

Each tactic has an associated cost. Once you get the tactics on the calendar, take a shot at what it will cost you to accomplish that tactic and then budget by strategy; i.e., the cost of a press kit, the cost of promotional materials. It's important that you discuss these things with your publisher. Since you already understand your contract, in detail, you know who is going to be paying for what—or, at least, what your sales and promotion budget will be. Approximately.

Do not expect to make any money the first year. That is, any profit. Like any product introduction, a book requires some up-front investment. Sorry to have to tell you that. But then, again, you're not in this for the money. Right?

I hope not.

One last thought before we move on. "Why," you may ask, "is putting all this in writing so important?"

Several reasons: First, discipline. Why do you think Santa makes a list and checks it twice? It's a good way to make sure you're attending to that all-important followthrough—in a timely fashion.

Second, when you get it all down in writing for the first time, then you can much better judge if it's rational. Even if it's possible. You can look at the calendar of tactics and make an intelligent assessment as to whether you are both able and willing to undertake and accomplish all those things.

Third, it helps break down what otherwise might seem to be too big a hill to climb into individual steps. It's much easier to get up a hill one step at a time. And it provides a constant sense of accomplishment that will spur you on. Yes, it will. I guarantee it.

Chapter 9: Plan to Succeed. Or You'll Surely Fail.

69

Finally, it gives you a report card on your progress—weekly. You will know if you are behind schedule, ahead of schedule, or right on. That measurement is vital to developing the discipline to be a good salesman of your product. More on tactics, with live examples, in the next chapter.

Exhibit F. The Press Kit

Some things you'll want to include in your press kit.

Exhibit G. Marketing Plan Outline

(Major Sections Only)

Although every company has its own format, these are generally accepted major sections of a marketing plan. What you will need to be concerned with involves only Part VII—The Annual Plan. Just for fun, though. Who do you think your competition will be? What kinds of activities and products grab off dollars that might otherwise be spent on books? I'll bet you can list at least twenty-five. There will be no exam.	I. Introduction and Purpose
	II. Background/Executive Summary
	III. The Product Today
	IV. Competitive Products
	V. The Market
	VI. Current Research
	VII. Annual Plan
	      Objectives
	      Strategies
	      Tactics
	      Timetable
	      Budget
	VIII. Conclusion

Exhibit H. Actual Schedule and Checklist

2003 Bookstore/ Event Signings

Date	Market	Bookseller or Event	Location	Confirmed	Stock Ordered	Units Sold
JANUARY						
17	San Antonio	Borders	Quarry	Yes	Yes	26
18	Austin	Borders	South Austin	Yes	Yes	27
					Total	**53**
FEBRUARY						
11	Wimberley	Wimberley Rotary	Casa Loma Rest.	Yes	Yes	9
15	Fredericksburg	Main Book Shop	Main Street	Yes	Yes	10
28	Houston	TPRA Convention	Marriott - Galleria	Yes	Yes	11
29	Houston	Borders	River Oaks	Yes	Yes	22
					Total	**52**
MARCH						
1 (AM)	Houston	TPRA Convention	Marriott- Galleria	Yes	Yes	5
1 (PM)	Houston	Borders	Stafford Store	Yes	Yes	32
8	Fredericksburg	Main Book Shop	Main Street	Yes	Yes	19
15	Dallas	Borders	Old Town	Yes	Yes	35
22	San Antonio	Borders	Selma	Yes	Yes	23
					Total	**114**
APRIL						
2-3	Houston	Texas Library Assn.	Brown Convention Ctr	Yes	Yes	30
4	Houston	Borders	Westheimer 6PM	Yes	Yes	8
5	Houston	Borders	Westheimer 1PM	Yes	Yes	20
6	Fredericksburg	Library's Friends	Public Library	Yes	Yes	6
12	Fort Worth	Borders	I-30 & Hulen	Yes	Yes	26
19	Fredericksburg	Main Book Shop	Main Street	Yes	Yes	18
26	Winnsboro	TC Center for Arts	200 Market Street	Yes	Yes	4
					Total	**112**
MAY						
10	Fredericksburg	Main Book Shop	Main Street	Yes	Yes	16
13	Waco	Barnes & Noble	Lakeview Store	Yes	Yes	4
30	Irvine, CA	Irvine Book Club	TBD	Yes	Yes	3
31/6-1	Los Angeles	Book Expo America	LA Convention Ctr	Yes	Yes	120★
	★ Comp Galleys				**Total**	**23**
JUNE						
7	Houston	Borders Meyerland	610W/Beechnut 1PM	Yes	Yes	11
13	San Antonio	Borders Quarry	Quarry Center 1PM	Yes	Yes	22

Use your computer's table-making capabilities to create a combination schedule and checklist. Don't automatically assume either the publisher or booksellers will follow through with details, such as ordering enough books for a signing. It's your responsibility. And it takes only minutes to do it right.

Chapter 9: Plan to Succeed. Or You'll Surely Fail.

71

Exhibit I. Bookseller Contact Form

BORDERS

Market	Store Location	Store Manager	AMM	Phone	E-mail
Austin	North–Research Blvd	Mary Adams	Holly King	210/555-5012	holly@bbs.com
	South–Lamar	Hope Sheridan	Holly King	Same	Same
Houston	River Oaks	Martin Burks	Charles Jones	713/555-7318	cjones@bsg.com
	Stafford	Lacy Stephens	Charles Jones	Same	Same
Dallas	Old Town	Bill Wright	Lee Park	972/555-4000	lee@bsg.com

BARNES & NOBLE

Market	Store Location	Store Manager	CRM	Phone	E-Mail
Austin	Round Rock	Zach Wilson	Pete Mays	512/555-9810	pete@bn.com
	Sunset Valley	Lea Delgado	Linda Torres	512/555-1212	linda@bn.com
	Westlake	Ty Smith	Pam Heinz	512/555-2345	pam@bn.com
Waco	Lakeview	Ezra Field	Carla Toms	254/555-5678	carla@bn.com

Create a simple data form to allow yourself to get in touch with retailers of your books quickly. Carry a hard copy with you unless you take a notebook computer everywhere you go. You never know when you'll have the opportunity to add a friend to your list. Think of them as friends. Always keep in mind that they owe you nothing, but you can make them money. Simple Selling 101. By the way, not all of the info above is correct. On purpose.

Exhibit J. Sales Tracking Form

Month	Samples, Comps	Direct Pub. Sales	Shipped to Distributors	Shipped to Booksellers	Minus Returns	Monthly Sales Totals
January						
February						
. . .						
Annual Totals						

Do the best job you can of keeping up with sales on a regular basis. Once-a-month updates will take only a few minutes. But a form like this may save you grief when it's time to figure your royalties.

Chapter 10

Stuff You'll Need. And Use.

Now you have a plan. And you almost have a book. Just a few more weeks and the gestation period will be over. It's time to turn our attention to some basic tactical tools—sales aids that will help you sell your book. And sell more copies of it.

Pre-production Announcement Mailer

The first tool you'll need to develop and deploy is a simple, attractive pre-release announcement mailer. Your publisher's sales department should help you put a nice one together. Most likely, you'll first mail it out to all your mailing lists. Without a lot of thought, you will be able to come up with substantial mailing lists—as many as several hundred people you know or have been associated with over the years. For simplicity's sake, segregate your mailing lists into manageable groupings: friends and relatives; business associates; clubs and organizations to which you belong.

Design it to be a self-mailer, one with an address panel. Be sure to include an order form with provisions for multiple credit cards for payment. The text should tell a bit about the book, and verbatim quotes from some of your reader panel members can be included, too.

This piece need not be expensive. Remember, you're sending it mostly to people who will know you, or at least recognize your name. An inexpensively produced, black-and-white mailer will suffice just fine. If you are planning to mail 1,500, for example, go ahead and order 2,500. You will find that you'll use it over and over—at least for the first year. And an extra thousand will cost almost nothing—only a few dollars.

Promotional Posters

Since the art for your cover is already on a zip drive at your publisher, the cost to run out oversized, color copies is negligible. If your book's dust cover is properly designed, an oversized version, run through a laminator for added sturdiness, will make a great poster. You'll want one that's about sixteen by twenty inches for distant visibility.

What will you do with these posters?

They have many uses: Mount a couple on pieces of foam core (available at any art supply store), add simple easel-backs, and you have stand-up signs for appearances and signings. Slightly reduced-sized versions make great point-of-sale pieces for bookstores and announcement posters for bookstore doors and windows. Don't forget to modify it for seasonal appearances: "Great gift idea for the holidays"; "Dad will love this for Father's Day"; "Groundhogs of the world recommend . . ."

Postcard Invitations

Once again, note that the dimensions of the front of your book, and your posters, are roughly proportional to a four-by-five-inch postcard. Just change the printer settings from vertical to landscape, tweak the art a bit, and *voila!* You've got a colorful postcard (blank on the back for imprinting timely messages and affixing address labels). They can be run through a good laser printer from time to time, as you need them. Send them out, geographically (of course), in advance of bookstore signings or events where you will be appearing and selling your books.

Some bookstore chains' area marketing managers (AMMs) or community relations managers (CRMs) will even send them out for you. All you have to do is send them the imprinted cards and e-mail

them your invitation list, formatted for laser printer labels. Avery ©
brand labels, among others, I'm sure, contain precise instructions for
formatting your lists for laser and bubble-jet printers.

Point is, almost all this, except licking the stamps, can be done
quickly and efficiently on a desktop computer, using art that already
exists on your publisher's zip drives.

While you may from time to time find a specialized need for an
additional promotional piece, the big three, reviewed above, used re-
peatedly and consistently, will serve virtually all your needs.

Remember one thing that's very important, though: Your publisher's sales department will be helping you by cranking out these
pieces for you. Do not—let me repeat that—*do not* make a habit of
calling them at the eleventh hour needing more posters, more postcards, more this, more that. You will almost never find yourself needing materials quickly if you plan ahead, monitor your plan, and follow up, follow up, follow up.

Then, on that rare occasion when you get an unplanned but great
opportunity at the last minute, the publisher's staff won't mind interrupting their planned work schedule to help you out. Once or
twice a year.

On-the-Fly Signing Kit

What you're about to read you will learn for yourself, the hard
way, after you've appeared at two or three events and done a couple
of store signings.

So, if you prefer to do things in the most difficult and painful
fashion, just skip right on over this next section. And take your licks
the first few times out on the hustings.

Since I, great guy that I am, had to learn by trial-and-error, ever
so painfully, at times, I'm willing to pass on the wisdom I scooped up
amid what was often a comedic, scrambling farce—at no extra charge
other than the measly amount you paid for this book.

Please consider that I'm trying to save you embarrassment, pain,
wasted time, and other assorted travails too macabre to even mention
with a little advice on what to take with you to events and signings.

I call this my "On-the-Fly Signing Kit." Here's what I have ready
to go at all times in two briefcases:

Chapter 10: Stuff You'll Need. And Use.

75

- *Eight to ten extra copies of your book.* Yes, I know the store is supposed to have ordered a case. Or the publisher is supposed to
have shipped two cases. Whatever. Fact is, things sometimes
slip through the cracks. If you have driven 319 miles to a big-
time book-selling opportunity, get there and find out somebody forgot to order your book—or the shipment got lost and
went to East Jesus instead of West Overshoe—well, then, my
well-prepared friend, you will be ever grateful for the fact
that I learned this lesson the hard way. And passed my wisdom on to you. Hallelujah.

  P.S.—It's *always* a good idea to carry a case of your books
  in the trunk of your car or behind the seat in your pickup. If
  you don't have 'em, you sure can't sell 'em. Enough said.
- *A tablecloth.* One about half the size of a standard folding table.
The kind everybody rents from Ducky Bob or Abby Rents.
You may need it only occasionally, but when you need it,
you'll need it. Why? Try working on top of an old rental table
that has "For a good time, call 555-5555" scratched about six
inches high and a half-inch deep in its surface.
- *Two easel-backed stand-up posters.* You may only have room at
your table for one. Or you may find yourself on a corner
where you have the opportunity to stop traffic from two different directions. Be prepared. Just in case. Remember, you
will want to maximize every opportunity.
- *A stack of your pre-release promotional flyers.* Slip one into every
book you sign and sell. Who knows? If the buyer really likes
Devil's Lust in the Dust Devils, he or she might just order additional copies for gifts. Remember, maximize every opportunity.
- *Signing invitation postcards.* These little babies are as handy as
wet-wipes in a rib restaurant. You just never know what you
might use them for. I guarantee you will find multiple uses
for them, on the spot. But if you don't have them? Well, figure it out.
- *Multiple felt-tip pens.* I like Sharpies ©. And no, Sanford, or
whoever makes them, didn't pay me to say that. Choose your
own brand. But, for heaven's sake, don't sign with a ballpoint
pen. How tacky! Unless, of course, it's the only thing available
and you'll lose a sale otherwise. *Hint:* If all else fails, prick your

finger and sign in blood. Never miss a sale. *Another hint:* These pretty good and inexpensive little Sharpies, or whatevers, come in multiple ink colors. Select a color that's complementary to the look of your book and the title page where you'll be signing. Ask your book designer. He or she will know.

- *Invisible tape.* You will use it. Somehow. Somewhere. At every event or signing. Trust me. It is indispensable. And comes in its own dispenser. Think about that one.
- *Scissors.* A good pair. Some that will cut thin cardboard and help you fabricate an as-yet-unheard-of and undiscovered miracle solution to on-the-spot problems as yet unheard of and undiscovered.
- *A good pocketknife.* I recommend the official Swiss Army knife. No, they didn't pay me either. But those little boogers will do just about anything or everything you may need done. Including remove the stringy, tough strands of chicken from between your teeth after another of those dreadful banquet lunches. Even open a bottle of cheap (but corked) wine when you've had about enough of this little foray and need a break. Physical and spiritual. *Hint:* If you are flying, forget the scissors and pocketknife. Unless you have some you want to get rid of—permanently.
- *A small first-aid kit.* Be sure it contains aspirin or other pain relievers, antacids, and maybe a small flask of Black Jack. Just to sterilize a potentially deadly paper cut, don't you see?
- *Your appearance schedule.* Most important you carry this with you. Invariably (or at least pretty often) you will get a chance to book another signing opportunity. It's best to be able to say on the spot when you're available. Remember, you're trying to maximize your opportunities.

That's it. The entire contents of your own little appearance kit. Give it whatever name strikes you, or at least one you can remember. But, like American Express, don't leave home without it.

Now that your appearance kit is ready to go, let's look at a few brand- and sales-enhancing things you can do prior to each appearance.

If you have not done so, provide a complete press kit to the area marketing manager or community relations manager at the book-

Chapter 10: Stuff You'll Need. And Use.

77

store chain where you will be signing. Get the name of the store manager whose store you will be visiting and send that person a brief note along with a signed and personalized copy of *Devil's Lust in the Dust Devils*. This little touch is called "sampling" in the vernacular of the marketing process. There is nothing sinister or illegal about it. It's not payola. It just makes good business sense.

In the same marketing vernacular, it is called "groveling." Every good salesperson knows when to grovel. In your case, "when" would be permanently until that particular store stocks your book and re-orders consistently. Even then, a sincere "Thank you" wouldn't harm your cause. Remember, just because you wrote a book and it some-how got published doesn't mean squat to the booksellers. If they don't want to stock your book, you are just plain out of luck. So, doesn't it make sense to demonstrate to them that you are a good per-son to work with and that your book, with your sales acumen, can make money for them?

Sure it does. But more about that in Chapter 12, in which we'll all learn to be humble.

Meantime, have you seen anything yet that looks particularly complicated? If you have, may I suggest you are overworking the issue. Taken in small steps and in an organized manner, the whole business of maximizing the potential of *Devil's Lust in the Dust Devils* can be learned, implemented, and eventually proclaimed a rousing success. At least compared to what would happen to you and your book if you just sat in a corner and waited for somebody else to do the selling for you.

Not gonna happen. Wouldn't be prudent.

That's the subject of the next chapter.

Exhibit K.
Pre-production Announcement Mailer

A simple, inexpensive mailer announcing the upcoming publication of your book not only can generate significant advance sales but also makes a useful ongoing promotional piece.

Exhibit L. Promotional Posters

Posters, easily and inexpensively crafted from the front of your dust cover, make excellent point-of-sale pieces: on easel-back stands at signings; on retailers' shelves below your books; even as window/door announcements at retail bookstores.

Exhibit M.
Postcard Invitations

Colorful postcards will have a variety of uses as you get into the groove of promoting and selling your book.

Chapter 10: Stuff You'll Need. And Use.

Exhibit N. Signing Kit Contents Checklist

Don't leave home without these things:

- An extra eight to ten copies of your book—just in case. Heck, carry a case of them in the trunk of your car.
- A small tablecloth.
- Two stand-up posters.
- Pre-release promotional flyers.
- Signing invitation postcards.
- Several felt-tip pens, color-coordinated with your book.
- Invisible tape.
- Scissors.
- Pocketknife.
- Minimal first-aid kit (including a flagon of medicinal Black Jack).
- Your updated appearance schedule.

Chapter 11

Sorry, Charley.
There Is No Pixie Dust.

In this chapter, we're going to take a cold, hard look at some of the cold, hard realities of the book production process—what it takes and how long it takes to produce a book, once you have the manuscript ready to turn in.

Along the way, we'll explore and debunk many of the common myths associated with the process. Things first-time and wannabe authors likely won't know, and even if they have a clue or two, won't want to admit.

Cold, hard reality: Producing (finished manuscript to product) a book takes time. Up to about six months. And the more you know and understand about the process, the less time you, the author of *Devil's Lust in the Dust Devils,* will waste.

Let me give you a parallel example.

Over the past forty years, my wife and I have "built" four different houses. By "built" I mean we have been the purchasers of houses to be built. How is this relevant? It takes about the same amount of time to produce a book from manuscript to finished product as it does to produce a house from blueprints to move-in day.

The first time out, for us, was an absolute nightmare. I found myself, at one point, with my hands around the builder's throat, attempting to choke him. Not that he didn't deserve to be choked, mind you, after trying, with a straight face, to convince me I would really like pink bricks, even though they were supposed to be gray. Seems the brickmasons had already laid about six courses all the way around the house—wrong color, wrong size, wrong texture. But murder, even for such a serious transgression, is not a good idea.

I needed some magic pixie dust to sprinkle on the whole process to make the ongoing aggravation go away.

Guess what?

There was no magic pixie dust for house-building anxiety removal.

The second house was a bit less painful because we bought it at the framing stage. Our biggest challenge was to select materials and colors for finish-out. I immediately looked for pixie dust, but there was still none available.

So, like the chicken I had become, I left all the selections to my wife—along with the care of three small children under the age of five. No sense risking a Murder-1 charge.

Still, there was no specialized pixie dust for the home buyer abuilding.

Since the second effort was so easy for me, I decided to take a larger role in the third effort. Big mistake. Total reversion—and revulsion—at the process. I ended up (gasp) in the office of an attorney, looking for remedies to get the builder to finish the house. It was like I had a book but no dust cover.

And still no pixie dust.

Fourth time around, I had finally learned a thing or two. Like, you can't rush the process. Just won't happen. And you don't have control over subcontractors or their schedules. We (*la signora ed io*) designed the house we wanted, got an architect to draw the construction plans, selected a very good and reputable builder, gave him some starting money, and then we got out of Dodge. Actually lived 250 miles away the entire time the house was being built, making only monthly two-day inspection trips.

Guess what? The process, carried out by e-mail and facsimile, with an occasional telephone call, was actually pleasant. Not once did we think about pixie dust. Didn't need it.

What are the lessons to be learned here as they relate to producing a book?

Simple.

Find a publisher you can trust and work with, give them the manuscript, cooperate with the editor, listen to and respect the book designer. Answer questions when asked. Check in occasionally. And mostly, just stay out of the way.

Spend your time concocting a devilishly clever marketing plan to brand your book and yourself and sell a boatload. Remember those six-plus billion potential buyers out there.

I know from sad experience that some of us are not as clever as Pavlov's dog. Or Mark Twain's cat. It was Mark Twain who said, wisely (and approximately), "Take care to get out of an experience only that wisdom which is worth learning. Not like the cat that once sits on a hot stove lid and will never again sit on a stove lid at all. Even if it's cold."

Perhaps my experience, both in building houses and in producing books (in the author's role only, you understand), will provide some comfort, guidance, and patience to your own future experiences. Producing books. Or building houses, for that matter. No extra charge for the construction process tips.

To help you get through the "six months from hell" while most of what's happening is completely beyond your control, we're going to take a look at some of the common misconceptions authors bring to the table. The myths, if you will, about book production. And we're going to have some fun (remember?) poking holes in those myths—punching the myth-balloons with a sharp pin. What comes out when those balloons explode will be worth remembering when it's your time to sit. And wait. In isolation. Alone and uninformed.

Got the picture?

Okay, here we go.

Common Myths

- It really doesn't take six months to produce a book. My god, a couple of industrious monks from the Dark Ages could whip out a dozen or so copies—using only goose quill pens.
- If my publisher's staff were more efficient and harder working, I could have a book in half the time.

Chapter 11: Sorry, Charley. There Is No Pixie Dust.

83

- If they would just let me get more involved, I could speed up the process. We could make final decisions on-the-fly and save tons of time.
- There are too many books in the publisher's house at one time. No wonder they can't concentrate on getting my book out. They have seven more right at the same stage, and a dozen waiting in line.
- None of these other books is going to sell as well as, or make as much money as, *Devil's Lust in the Dust Devils.* Can't these people see that? And put first things first?
- I may go broke waiting to sell these books. Six months is a long time to wait for my paycheck.

We could go on and on with these myths. You can think of many more. Just make a list of all the things you expect will happen during the production process, and then label that page "Myths." Right at the top. In big, bold letters. Italics, even.

But these six are enough to make all the points that need to be made to prepare you for your half-year of isolation. So you can make the most of this (mostly) down-time, concentrating on getting ready to be your own marketer, promoter, and salesman.

Let's look at these common misconceptions, all of which have to do with "patience," or lack thereof, one at a time.

It really doesn't take six months to produce a book.

Yes, it does. At least. But why? Well, we've already talked about the editing process and the book designing process—and your roles in both of those. Once the editor starts, he or she will need at least two weeks. If your manuscript is clean. If you have taken the input from your reader panel to heart and eliminated the redundancies, the factual glitches, the contextual faux pas.

In short, if you turn in a really good manuscript that's already been through the reader process and your own two or three waves of edit, you'll still need a couple of weeks for the editor to do a good job. Minimum.

If, on the other hand, your manuscript has been written over three or five years, or you ignored the input from your reader panel, or you just gave it a once-over last-read yourself, you must double that time. At least.

Point? The more you do to get the manuscript ready up front, the less effort the editor will have to expend. And less effort requires less time. Do not concern yourself that your editor might be dragging his or her feet. You can bet there are six or seven more manuscripts piled up to be edited. Just waiting. And editors are not paid by the hour, but by the volume of throughput. So, if your manuscript is a mess, you're costing your editor money. And yourself time.

If my publisher's staff were more efficient and harder working, I could have a book in half the time.

There may be a smidgen of truth to this mostly off-base thought process. But not enough to gain you more than a day or two. Your book designer, depending on the length of your manuscript, will need two to four weeks to properly design your book. Remember the individual flakes of corn in the fifteen-ounce box? That's the way it's done. They have no magic pixie dust either.

Facts are that one person, whether it's an editor or a book designer, can only work on one project at a time. Once they start with your manuscript, you are theirs until they're finished. If you seek to constantly interrupt them with questions or requests for status reports, you're burning your own time. And wasting theirs.

Point? Be available. Be prompt in responding. Be helpful. Run their errands for them. Gather the materials they need. And be prepared to make decisions quickly. Otherwise, you are just costing yourself time.

If they would just let me get more involved, I could speed up the process.

In the now-humorous words of my dear, departed mother-in-law, "What?!! Are you crrr-azy?" Stand by. You will be asked to participate when your participation will speed up the process. Trust me on that one. If you are pleasant to work with and don't waste their time, your publisher's staff will call on you when you can help them speed up the process. Or make the product better.

Chapter 11: Sorry, Charley. There Is No Pixie Dust.

85

That's it. Only two reasons. Ever.

For no other reasons will they seek to get you involved. They already know you can't edit your own manuscript. And they know you're not a book designer. How could you help them do those jobs?

Besides, you are supposed to be working, feverishly, on your marketing, branding, and salesmanship. Yes, I am harping on that point. Why? Because it's not as much fun to do as hanging around the publisher's offices and kibitzing (i.e., "getting in the way"). We all have a natural tendency to gravitate to where the fun action's going on.

Don't do it. Speak only when spoken to. After you have listened first, of course.

There are too many books in progress.
No wonder mine's taking so long.

The fact that *Devil's Lust in the Dust Devils* is only one of eight titles being edited and designed at one time is (are you ready for this?) to your advantage.

How can that be?

To take an extreme example, if your book were the only one the publisher was working on, they'd be out of business before it was ever finished. Publishing books is, at best, a crapshoot endeavor. Nobody (no pixie dust, remember) has yet been able to predict which titles will become million sellers. Or which will become huge bonfires. Especially works by first-time authors. Your publisher is really rolling the dice. If you do your part, as we're talking about in this book, your chances—and theirs—are greatly enhanced.

Let me relate a brief story to you. It may be urban myth. Or it may be true. It is told in writers' circles as fact.

Tom Clancy could not get any publisher, anywhere, to consider his first book, *The Hunt for Red October*. Finally, almost in desperation, he paid the U.S. Naval Academy Press to print a few thousand copies. And the rest, as those given to speaking tritely are wont to say, is history.

What does that tell you?

It tells me two things: First, it's hard as hell for a first-time author to get his or her manuscript turned into a book. And second, publishers are very careful to try to avoid "turkeys"—books that will languish on the shelves, only to be returned to the publisher from book-sellers for credit. And end up in a bonfire.

So, my impatient (but quick-learning) friend, be glad your publisher is working on many titles at once. Be joyful that they're smart enough to cover their backside in case one or two in the pipeline turn out to be "turkeys." Just don't let yours be one of them.

None of these other books is going to sell as well as, or make as much money as, mine.

Oh, yeah? If you can prove that, and if you're consistently able to pick manuscripts that will sell well in book form, I have a suggestion for you: Give up writing. Get a job screening manuscripts for publishers. Charge a percentage of the gross sales margin for every winner you pick.

You'll be not only an instant hero in the publishing industry, but you'll also be rich. As Croesus.

I may go broke waiting six months for my first paycheck.

Who in the world told you that you would get money when the book is finished? Not your contract. Re-read the fine print.

Fact is, if you are expecting a payday from your book, better plan on the first one being almost a year after your book's released.

Most publishers "settle-up" with authors only twice a year. That would be semi-annually. And the settlement for the volume sold between July 1 and December 31 of last year will not be ready to distribute before March or April of the following year.

"Why so long?" I can sense your impatience reaching new heights. Because, although your publisher and you will know how many units have been shipped, at what prices, immediately after December 31, there are two other factors that affect the timing of your payday.

First, the dreaded returns. In case you were not aware, booksellers are not inclined to take big risks. If they order sixty copies of *Devil's Lust in the Dust Devils* in early November for the holiday season, and they find they still have fifty-six of them come December 31, guess what's about to happen? They're going to send at least forty-eight of them back to the publisher—for credit. They will not pass "Go," but

Chapter 11: Sorry, Charley. There Is No Pixie Dust.

87

they will collect $804.96 in credit for what they paid for the forty-eight they're sending back. And you, my friend, have just lost a small chunk of what you thought you already had "in the bank."

Second reason for the delay is, guess what? Good thinking. Your publisher has to collect for the books shipped during the six months between July 1 and December 31 in order for them to be able to pay you and their other authors. And that takes time. Most booksellers will pay in sixty to ninety days from date of shipment. So those books shipped in December may not be paid for before the Ides of March. (*Et tu, Brute?*)

You need to know these things if you are planning to spend your royalties on anything significant. Like survival.

Enough of this "errant pedantry," as Winston Churchill was reputed to have said. You've got the point: Spend your time, while your book is being produced, getting ready to sell.

If you don't yet feel like you're ready to sell, that's fine. We're not through with that yet.

Because nothing happens until a sale is made. And there's no such thing as magic pixie dust.

"Don't look for divine intervention or the sudden appearance of a real salesman. You are *the salesman. Get over it. Just do it."*

Part V

And Nothing Happened 'til a Sale Was Made.

Chapter 12

The Pen Isn't Really So Mighty.

Are you starting to feel just a little bit humble yet?

Good.

I don't mean to suggest that you shouldn't be proud to be a writer. Or be proud that you have actually completed a major manuscript. After all, not everybody has done that. Not everybody *could* do that. And, of those who could, most have neither the desire nor the discipline to see such a lengthy process through to a successful conclusion.

Besides, there are probably too many people who are trying to do it but have neither the talent nor the discipline to make it happen. At least with any quality or redeeming value. Right?

So you have a right to stand tall. To be proud.

Just don't get carried away. Or too full of yourself.

Still, unlike Grog of 24,000 B.C., you have some help—some tools besides rocks and sticks. Unlike Shakespeare, you have inexpensive paper, by the ream. Unlike Agatha Christie, you haven't written eighty-four novels on a manual typewriter. The same machine on which you compose your unique and special combinations of words and phrases will, switched almost instantly to an alternate mode, help you do your research. Check facts. Verify dates. Even suggest corrections to your spelling and grammar. (My editor would like to remind you that often these suggested changes are wrong. So watch out.)

Anyway, you have done something most people will never do. Pat yourself on the back. Lightly.

Okay, feel-good time and the mini-pep rally are over. Back to reality. Tactical reality.

Where are you going to get those materials we talked about as part of your marketing plan and your sales kit? Remember, you'll need a pre-release announcement mailer to send out six weeks or so before *Devil's Lust in the Dust Devils* is released. And a couple of posters, some postcard invitations, and a whole bunch of stuff for your on-the-fly sales kit.

The time to begin working on these items is far in advance of the delivery date of your finished book.

How do you go about getting started?

Remember, we said that your publisher's sales department should help you produce these materials. Inexpensively. Most of the graphics you'll need already reside on zip drives in their offices.

But there is an efficient and sensible way to approach the process of getting these materials ready for your bag of tricks. And it involves some more discipline on your part.

Here's what I would suggest to maximize your materials' acquisition process and minimize wasted time for yourself and your publisher's sales and production departments.

Once you have a pretty good draft of your marketing plan with most of the "big five" categories completed (except for your budget, which will be fairly incomplete at this point), make an appointment with the person in your publisher's sales department who will be responsible for your title—among fifteen or twenty others, likely. Ask for about ninety minutes for the meeting. Then "present" the plan to that person—as if you were making a sales call. Really. It's good practice for selling time that's coming. And it will be the fastest way to convey your planned efforts to your sales contact. Plan to leave a draft copy with that person.

During that meeting, encourage an open exchange about which of you is going to be responsible for what activities. For example, your sales rep may suggest that you deal, at first, with independent booksellers in X, Y, and Z markets—probably smaller markets at first. And let the publisher's sales department work on the major chain booksellers in two or three bigger markets.

Why is that a good strategy? Because you, as a neophyte, need the practice of making multiple sales calls, for one thing. You can get that practice, as well as put a couple of local, smaller-scale signing appearances under your experience umbrella before being unleashed in a big store in a big market. And your publisher's sales rep is experienced in these kinds of activities already. He or she knows the right contacts. And he or she knows you, by now.

Whether specific, overt consideration is discussed (to try to match your personality or "brand," as well as the subject matter of your book, with specific chains or stores), that is exactly what an experienced publisher's sales department will do. They want you to get off to a good start. And they know neither you, nor they, can afford an early major embarrassment in any given bookseller chain. The word will get around to "watch out for" you among the AMMs or CRMs in that chain, and you will be dead meat. Road-kill in training.

Together, then, decide how you are going to attack signing and appearance schedules. Your rep will be able to enhance, even short-cut your efforts by giving you a list of events at which a selling opportunity will be available for local authors. These events—festivals, fairs, rodeos, Oktoberfests—are legion. And they are great places to hone your skills as an assertive (not aggressive) salesperson for your own book.

More about how to sell in the last chapter, "Where the Rubber Meets the Road."

Now that you have figured out who is going to attack which areas of in-store signings and personal appearances, what about those sales materials you're going to need?

That's the second half of the meeting.

Your plan will detail, or at least list, the various sales tools we discussed a few pages back. Start with the "big three"—the pre-release announcement mailer, the in-store poster/point-of-sale pieces, and the invitation postcards. Since your book designer has likely already finished with at least a rough comprehensive of the front cover of your book, that artwork is already on a zip drive or diskette.

Talk with your sales contact about what you expect to need. Discuss quantities (remember to order about twice as many pre-release announcement flyers as you expect to mail). Your marketing plan should already have detailed the first three or four seasonal variations of your poster art, depending on the time of year of the release. So you should, together, be able to decide, just for example, something like this:

Pre-release Announcements

Print 3,000 by what date?
Initial mailing 1,500 on what date?
Future use 1,500

In-Store Posters/Point-of-Sale Pieces

For signings
Introductory versions 2 by what date?
First-use seasonal 2 by what date?

For bookstore P-O-S
Introductory versions 12 by what date?
First seasonal version 12 by what date?

Postcard Invitation Shells

Introductory versions 750 by what date?
First seasonal version 250 by what date?

Remember, though these numbers are, more or less, realistic, the actual quantities will be determined in discussion with your sales department representative. Defer to that person's experience. He or she has done this hundreds of times. You're just cutting your teeth.

Also, use this opportunity to plug some costs into the budget portion of your marketing plan. Your sales contact will be able to tell you, approximately, the cost of the above quantities (or any quantities, for that matter) of the "big three" materials. Since the basic art has been created for the dust cover, costs will be surprisingly low—given today's magic, pixie dust-like computer technology.

You already know who is paying for the materials, right? Because you have made it your business to understand your contract. Of course you have. A long time ago.

What about the press kit? Who is going to write and prepare the materials? Who is going to control the distribution, as well as the timing of the distribution?

As my old great-grandmother used to say, "That's the third half of the meeting." And it won't take long.

First, you already know what's in the kit. Second, you are a writer. Third, you are really, really close to both the product and the author—which can be a real negative.

Here's my suggestion. Take a crack at a draft of the various inserts: the general announcement news release; the author's bio; a clever but short feature story relating to the theme of the book. Then, because you are so close to the manuscript, the story, and to yourself, let your editor critique it. Give the finished drafts to your publisher's sales department, and let them be responsible for the distribution of press kits. Just to avoid an embarrassing duplication, don't you see? Besides, they know the book editors and how to reach them.

When you need a kit sent to a broadcast producer or an entertainment editor or anybody else, just let your publisher's representative know by e-mail. Chances are, the kit will go out the same day.

So that's it. You have done it. You have created a plan. And you have begun to work that plan. You are keeping your publisher informed and in the loop. And you are being open to listening and learning.

Just as I promised. Without magic.

Before we close out this discussion, I want to hit you one more time with the idea that this all should be FUN. If it is not, perhaps you're working too hard at it—overworking the problem, so to speak. The only counsel I can give you is to relax. Decide up front that this whole business of learning to become your own promoter and salesperson is going to be an enjoyable learning experience.

Then do everything you can to make it fun.

Exhibit O. Order of the Action–Manuscript to Finished Product

One More 12-Step Program

1. Form your reader panel and do the preliminary research on your product.
2. Do the first edit yourself, based on feedback from your reader panel.
3. Research potential publishers; select a "most likely" group.
4. Research the peculiar requirements of each publisher's submission guidelines. Comply. Precisely.
5. Sell your manuscript based on the "smarts" you've gathered in your research. And clearly understand the details of your contract.
6. Cooperate with and respect the editor.
7. Cooperate with and respect the book designer.
8. Develop your own mini-marketing plan, featuring the "big five." Define your brands—yours and your book's.
9. Meet with your publisher's sales department to carve up responsibilities and get sales materials produced. Stay in touch with them. Regularly.
10. Begin your sales calls in cooperation with and in conjunction with your publisher's sales department.
11. Practice. Practice. Practice your sales techniques.
12. Go forth and sell a boatload of *Devil's Lust in the Dust Devils.*

Total elapsed time: Fifteen to twenty-two months.

Chapter 13

Retailers Don't Owe You
the Time of Day.

How many times, as you were struggling through the fourteenth draft of a particularly difficult chapter, did you think to yourself, *If I can just get this manuscript finished and sold, I'm over the hump—every bookseller in the Southwest is going to just have to stock it and sell it.*

Wrong!

As the title of this chapter suggests, not so subtly, booksellers do not automatically order, stock, display, and sell every book that comes along. They pick and choose based on their own assessment of what they think will sell in their stores—and which authors and publishers will help them sell enough volume to make some real money. They are not lending libraries, after all.

In the bookselling business, the name of the game is *profit*. Not "support your local author."

What does that suggest to you? That perhaps you'd better be ready to sell? First to the booksellers? And then to their customers?

Good. You're getting the picture. The cold, hard reality.

So, now that you are armed with the wisdom of the preceding chapters, how do you approach the challenge of selling your book to the book trade? And then, how do you approach selling the book to the customers of that book trade? Those are the two burning questions we'll be answering in the next two chapters.

Unless you are by now committed, unless you are chomping at the bit, unless you just can't wait to get at the selling process, you'll probably never do much better than break even.

Financially speaking. If you even do that.

Cold, hard reality.

For those true believers who are ready to become salespersons, let's charge forward. Because we are finally in the home stretch of all the things you need to know to be a best-selling author.

Let's begin at the beginning of the sales cycle. Notice I did not say "sales process." The process began the minute you sat down to outline your great American novel. Long ago.

Now, though, you are weeks away from a finished product. Your publisher will likely be able to arm you with what are called "bound galleys." They look like oversized paperback books. Your colorful cover will be wrapped around what will likely not yet be completely finished insides. Not to worry, though. The booksellers know what these little gems are. And now they know that you're getting close, very close, to a finished book.

As we discussed some time back, if this is your first book (or at least the first one you've committed to sell, yourself, because you are now enlightened), it will probably be a good idea for you to start out calling on the smaller, independent booksellers in smaller markets. Leave the big guys, just initially, to your publisher's sales department.

For our purposes, it doesn't matter whether you are calling on the sole proprietor of Ajax Independent Book Sales in West Overshoe, Idaho, or the presidents of the big, national chain stores. What you will need to know, and do, is identical. How you will need to prepare is the same. The mindset you will need to adopt is no different.

So, here we go.

What is the first, second, third, and last thing a bookseller cares about?

Making a profit.

Good thinking. You are learning something here, I can tell.

So on what terms and with what mindset are you going to approach Pierre Ajax when you call on him in West Overshoe?

Of course, you are going to begin, and end, your conversation with him by demonstrating how you are going to help him make more money if he chooses to stock your book. You are going to convince him that you are willing to do all the things it takes to sell a boatload of books in his store.

What are those things?

- First, you are going to be exhibiting your personal brand. You may even be "in character." Dressed as Little Joe Cartwright in *Little House on the Prairie*. (Don't worry. My editor will catch this mix-up.) [Editor's note: Michael Landon starred in *LHOTP*, but his character Little Joe was featured in the TV show *Bonanza*. Thanks, George, for the extra work.]
- You are going to start your conversation, after introducing yourself and handing him a copy of your press kit, by saying something like, "I am absolutely committed to selling a boatload of *Devil's Lust in the Dust Devils*. Personally."
- You are going to show him your point-of-sale posters and tell him they will be provided with each order of six or more books.
- You are going to show him your postcards and tell him that every time he will allow you to come into his store, as a guest, and sell and sign your books, you will send out at least fifty invitations into his retail trade area—to draw more people into the store. Even if they don't buy your book, you will opine, once they're in the store, there is an opportunity to sell them something. "Traffic's the name of the game," you will state, as if you have studied retailing at the feet of Stanley Marcus for twenty years.
- You are then going to say something like, "I am an assertive salesperson. I know how to sell, and I will move a ton of books. Besides, I like signings to go on for six to eight hours. None of those two-hour mini-gigs for me."

    And then you will smile, knowingly, like the Cheshire Cat that ate the canary. (Note to editor: Did the Cheshire Cat in *Through the Looking Glass* eat a canary?) [Editor's note: I don't think anyone cares. Let's move forward here. Okay?]

- Then you are going to pull out your schedule and suggest two or three alternate days and dates for an in-store signing. You are not going to meekly ask if you can come in and do a signing. You are going to assume the answer to that is "yes," just giving old Pierre the chance to select a date.

   Make a note to yourself: Where do you come up with fifty or more names and addresses in a strange (to you) market? Someplace where you don't really know a soul? Start with the bookseller. That's one. Then check references in the Yellow Pages and in the local library for organizations, such as writers' groups. Don't forget English teachers at the local high schools. Add others who would be interested in the subject matter of your book. For *Devil's Lust in the Dust Devils,* you might want to include teachers of history. These lists are easy to obtain once you've had a bit of practice.

You will be amazed how receptive most of these independent booksellers will be.

And why is that?

Because they will immediately see that you have their best interests in mind. That you really *do* want to make them some money. And yourself and Earthy Publications LLP, too. Nothing wrong with that. As long as you put the booksellers first.

Then, when you get the date agreed to and on your schedule, what do you do next?

Shut up and get the hell out of there. With nothing more than a "Thank you very much" and a gracious "Good-bye."

Do NOT stand around talking. Do NOT keep selling. Your bookseller is convinced. He has said "Yes" and given you a date. Nothing good can happen if you keep talking—only bad things. This may be the hardest lesson to get across to neophyte salespeople.

Once the customer agrees, SHUT UP AND GET OUT!

You will become excited at a successful sale (yes, you will!) and have the urge to babble on, spouting incoherent platitudes.

Don't do it.

Leave.

That's it. Not difficult. Not magic. Simple, simple, simple.

And being in character makes it much easier than you might

imagine. Remember, you will not be yourself—probably a shy, al-most-afraid-of-people introvert who writes books. You will be Little Joe, or whoever that guy was. You, yourself, don't have to face rejection. It won't be you being rejected (won't happen too often, but you will run into it). It will be a character from the nineteenth century, or whatever character you have adopted.

And those people never took rejection personally. Right?

Voila! You are now a salesperson. Or, at least, your alter ego from 110 years ago is a salesperson. Good work!

Fast forward a couple of months.

You have now successfully set up a series of signings in independent booksellers and you are getting better at the processes—both selling to the trade and selling to the consumers on the retail sales floor. In marketing terms, you're "moving the tonnage." It's time for you to venture into the big-time world of chain booksellers.

Does that frighten you?

Relax.

What you will be doing is no different from what you already have been doing with the independents. And doing quite successfully by now.

The only thing that's a little different is the stakes. It's okay if you screw up and get thrown out of Pierre Ajax's store, never to be allowed on the same side of the street again, by town ordinance. But do that with one area marketing manager or one community relations manager or one store manager in a major bookseller chain, and the word will spread within that company. And within its competitors.

Bookselling is a small fraternity, after all.

But not to worry. That's why you "earned your spurs" in the independent bookseller arena. Remember: These people gave you your start. Never walk away from them. Keep selling and supporting the independents.

So, let's talk a bit about approaching big bookseller chains.

Approaching Pierre was easy. He was the sole proprietor. He manages the inventory. He orders for the store. He makes all the decisions. Not so simple when you get into the chains. But not complicated, either.

I promise.

Let's pause here to take a look at the players in a typical bookseller chain. Who they are. What they are variously called. Who does what. And who matters to you, the now great seller of books. And, of course, how you deal with each of them—based on their responsibilities and needs.

Typically there are five different individuals associated with each store in some manner. Five people who will accept or reject *Devil's Lust in the Dust Devils.* And its author.

Starting at the decision-making level, as far as you're concerned, the most important person will be the one variously called *area marketing manager* or *community relations manager* or something similar, depending on which chain you're approaching.

This is the person who will say "Yes" or "No" to in-store signings and appearance opportunities.

For the sake of simplicity, and because of the various titles associated with this function, let's just call this person *My Best Friend,* or MBF for short. Get it?

Who is this person and what does he or she do?

The MBFs usually have several stores for which they are responsible, often in more than one major market. MBFs are the people who arrange for, orchestrate, and pull off activities and programs designed to position their stores and their chains as "experts" among the literati, that portion of the population who are already predisposed to read, write, teach—in short, who give a hoot about books and the people who write them.

So MBFs arrange for events with authors. Educators. Book clubs. And, yes, for the in-store signings in each of the stores for which they are responsible.

MBFs are your point-of-entry into a major bookseller. They often determine, by default, whether your book is stocked in a particular store. Whether it gets special display treatment. Whether you are allowed to come in, as their guests, to sell it from time to time.

MBFs are busy. Their plates are full. So, given the choice between a passive author who thinks they owe him or her the chance to participate in a signing—with no preparation, understanding, cooperation or particular effort—and you, the savvy bookseller who moves the tonnage, who do you think will rise to the top of the schedule? And get the best retail days? And the preferences for gift-giving holiday signings?

Bingo!

To build a positive relationship with MBFs, there are just a few simple things you need to know:

- Booksellers don't "owe" you a damned thing. Period. End of discussion.
- You owe the booksellers, and especially the MBF, the following:

A *willingness to listen.* And learn.

An *invitation mailing list* of at least fifty persons in their trade area.

Postcards to send to that list inviting them to a signing. And a willingness to send those postcards out on your own. (It's the MBF's choice. Some prefer to handle the mailing themselves. Others want you to do it. Just ask.)

Posters and point-of-sale materials with which to both promote your appearance and call attention to your book's display.

A *willingness to show up on time, work hard, and stay long.* In other words, to sell a bunch of books.

Accessibility and flexibility. Quick response to their inquiries and needs, in other words.

Respect (there's that word again) for their needs to do their job better. Or even get it done at all.

What's the best way to get into the good graces of MBFs? And stay there?

Simple: Sell a bunch of books when you have the opportunity for a signing. Remember? Profit is the name of the game. Starting with the MBFs.

You may not be aware that the national average number of sales for an in-store signing is *less than five.*

That's right.

Only four-plus. And that includes the mega-sellers, like Clancy, who will move hundreds.

Think about that. Amazing.

Why is that? Because most authors, withdrawn introverts that they are, sit behind a table with a stack of books, passively looking down, not in any particular character, almost seeking to avoid eye contact or conversation with a dreaded customer who might buy a book.

You've seen it. Maybe even done it.

The author behind that table might as well be a mannequin.

If you go into a signing, armed with your "on-the-fly" sales kit, dressed to convey your personal brand, and willing to be assertive, to seek out your targets, get their attention, engage them in conversation and—most important—give them quick and intelligent reasons why they should buy your book, then, guess what?

You will sell four to five books an hour! I guarantee it.

If you are willing to stay six or seven hours and sell twenty-five to thirty books, you are going to absolutely amaze your MBF. And all the other four cast members we're about to introduce to you.

You walk out of that store having sold more than a case of books, and you have made a statement. To wit: "I walk the walk. I move the tonnage."

And you will be invited back. Again and again. And invited quickly into the other stores that same MBF is responsible for. On the best sales days with the greatest floor traffic. You will even find that impressing the MBFs by just doing what I contend is your job—selling the hell out of your book—will result in MBFs bidding to get you scheduled for the Fridays and Saturdays before Mother's Day. Father's Day. St. Swithen's Day (look it up).

Success breeds success. And you'll be on your way. Guaranteed.

Even (gasp) if your book is not the greatest thing since Houdini drowned. [Editor's note: Tony Curtis portrayed Houdini drowning. But Houdini actually died from peritonitis in a hospital.]

Who are the other players in the book chains who are important for you to know and grovel before? Initially, at least.

The next most important person in the pecking order will be the person who actually decides which books, and how many, to order and stock. And whether to restock. Or (shudder) return. These people go by various titles, depending on which chain we're looking into, but you need to be a hero to them as well. For the sake of simplicity, call them MSBFs—*My Second Best Friends.*

You will have little interface with these people. Just sell a boatload of books, generate some traffic, and ("Here he goes, again, Mabel") generate some fun in the store at your signing opportunities, and they will come to you.

And reorder your books.

And display them prominently.

You win. Again.

The next person to get to know and appreciate is the store's *general manager* (GM). By all means, introduce yourself to that person when you arrive at the store and hand over a complimentary copy of your book, personalized and signed. Make it clear that it is for their private collection, not for resale in the store. Thank that GM for the opportunity to be a guest in his or her store, and commit to sell a bunch of books for them—to make them some money.

Look at it this way. If you sell thirty copies on a Saturday, what have you done for that GM? You have increased gross sales by $838.50. You have added $335.40 to his or her gross margin for the day. And as much as $50.00 to the net profit of that store for the day.

All incremental dollars.

That's not peanuts.

You are now a hero. And you're welcome to come back. Over and over. Your book will get preferential treatment when it comes to those bookstore lists of recommended titles, too.

In short, success continues breeding success.

Another person important to your success, particularly on the day you're doing the signing, is called the *floor manager* (FM). That's the person in charge of the store at the moment. He or she is likely the person who will greet you and set you up in your station for the day. And the person you will seek out if you have questions or need something while you are there. Get acquainted with the FM. Promise to sell a bunch of books (notice how we keep repeating this commitment to everyone associated with the retail side?). Then do it.

Finally, there's the "big cheese" (BC)—the *regional manager for the chain* who is responsible for the sales and operation of a dozen or more stores in multiple markets, often in more than one state. The BC almost always offices in what are called "flagship" stores in big cities. When the MBF schedules you for a signing in the store where the BC offices, immediately (do not pass "Go," do not collect $200) send that BC a letter, anticipating the pleasure of meeting him or her on the day you'll be there. Enclose a signed and personalized copy of your book.

And when you get to the store, inquire if the BC (better use the title "regional manager") is on the premises. So you can pay your respects, don't you see? And grovel before the top dog. For sure.

If you are making the BC's stores money, he or she will want to at least say "Hello" to you. Make the most of this opportunity. Know what other markets the BC is responsible for and inquire as to when you might have the pleasure of making the stores in East Jesus, Wyoming, some money, too.

Never miss the chance to book another event or signing.

Well, that's about it for the bookseller relationship lessons. The whole process is nothing more than creative selling.

Now you know who is important to the success of *Devil's Lust in the Dust Devils* among independent booksellers and major chains.

Go get 'em.

And, oh, yes. Be sure to have some fun while you're at it!

Exhibit P. Checklist for a Bookstore Signing

Three weeks in advance:

- Contact the appropriate MBF. Get the names of the store GM and MSBF. Ask if the MBF wants to send the invitations or wants you to send them. Suggest an appropriate number of books that should be ordered by the MSBM for the signing.
- Add the GM and MSBF to your contact database list.
- Send the MBF a signed, personalized copy of your book.
- Prepare your invitation mailing list, formatted for self-adhesive labels.
- Contact your publisher's sales department. Give them your schedule and request they prepare an appropriate number of postcard overprinted invitations.

Two weeks in advance:

- Be sure the postcards have arrived—either with the MBF or with you.
- If the MBF is mailing the postcards, e-mail your formatted mailing list to him or her.
- If you are mailing the postcard invitations, run off the labels and lick the stamps and mail them.
- Ask your publisher's sales representative to send appropriate posters and point-of-sale pieces to the MBF.

- Send a personal letter and invitation to attend the signing, along with a sample copy of *Devil's Lust in the Dust Devils,* to book editors and other media representatives in the region of the signing. Or ask your publisher's sales department to do this. However the two of you have decided to proceed.

One week in advance:
- Check to see that the posters have arrived and the postcards have been mailed, if the MBF is mailing them. The appropriate inquiry is, "Have you received everything you need? Do you need anything more from me?"
- Get precise directions to the store. Do not—I repeat, *not*—be late because you can't find the place. Inexcusable. Unforgivable. Inadmissible.
- Check with your publisher's sales department to see if the books for the signing have been ordered yet by the MSBF. If not, contact the MBF and offer to bring them to the signing with you. (Note: If you do bring them, be sure to get a purchase order number and give that information to your publisher's sales department immediately so the bookseller can be invoiced, by facsimile—since they already have the books.)
- Replenish the supplies in your "on-the-fly" sales kit. Be sure it's ready to fly with you.
- Be sure your wardrobe is clean and ready—your 1890s dress and bloomers if you are female (or slightly kinky) or your jeans, chaps, and shirt, if you are male. Or female, for that matter.
- Practice. Practice. Practice.

Immediately following:
- Report your results to the MBF and your publisher's sales department.
- Suggest to your MBF that, based on your sales record, it would be a good idea to go ahead and book you into a couple more stores. Now's the time to keep after additional opportunities.
- Suggest to your MSBF that it would be a good idea to order some additional copies. Invariably, the store where you sign will move additional inventory over the next two to three weeks— if those who bought your book like it as much as you do.

Chapter 13: Retailers Don't Owe You the Time of Day.

- Send "thank you's" to those who helped make your successful selling experience possible.
- Record your results on your inventory tracking forms and on your schedule form.
- Sit down with a clean piece of paper and think. Think of what you did that you might do better next time. Think of changes to your approach that might help you sell a couple more books. Ask yourself if you are becoming stale in some aspects of your presentation. Should you back off and listen more? Never stop trying to improve, no matter how good you get.

You can always lose your edge. Or get better. It's your choice.

Where the Rubber Meets the Road.

If you are over the age of fifty, you probably know the origins of the headline to this final chapter. For you tadpoles, I will tell you it is one of the greatest advertising lines ever written—about a half century ago for a major tire company.

Six words that say all there is to say.

I spent more than thirty years in the advertising agency business—as a writer, a pin-striped account guy, a public relations guru, and, finally, as president of a very creative agency for twenty-two years. Try as I might, I never wrote a headline as good as the title of this chapter. Or at least not one that has become a part of everyday English lexicon.

I always tell people my greatest writing was done in Portuguese. Not that I really write or understand a word of that language, mind you. But so few others do that I have found I can grunt out a few lilting syllables, punctuated—as in music—by vowels in cadence, and others think I'm really speaking a foreign language.

Probably some language even more obscure would be still more convincing. Something like Latvian. Or Swahili. Who would know?

What's the point? Just this: There's a certain amount of luck at play when something truly memorable is written for the first time. But it would never rise to the heights of memorability unless someone, somehow, sold it. And remember this well: There is a degree of showmanship inherent in the process of selling and being memorable while you're at it.

That sound familiar?

Good.

Let's get on with finishing up our last, simple lesson in salesmanship. What happens on the retail sales floor, where the rubber meets the road?

In this chapter, we're going to take a close look at how you go about maximizing your sales opportunities during those precious few hours when a bookseller hands over a folding table, a folding chair, and about eight square feet of floor space to you. You will learn how to get yourself noticed by potential customers as they enter the store. How to approach potential customers without folding, yourself. How to decide which potential customers to approach—and which to forget about. How to engage the real prospects among them in a dialogue that will allow you to give them reasons to buy your book that are meaningful to them. How to toss in a little showmanship that will mean the difference between a sale and a waste of precious time. Even how to read a customer's propensity to buy by being keenly observant. And looking him or her straight in the eye.

It's all called "one-on-one salesmanship." Or "personal selling."

The quicker you learn it, the more books you will sell. And the more opportunities you will have to sell more books. Remember: Success breeds success.

So, let's get going. What does it take to become a great one-on-one salesman?

First things first. Make yourself conspicuous.

It's a lead-pipe cinch you will never sell a book to a bookstore customer who never sees you. Right?

Oh, sure, your FM will set you up right near the front door. (If they don't, ask politely to move. That's where the action is. Trust me.) Still, within a few minutes you will find it amazing how many people are either so preoccupied or on such a focused mission that they just do not even notice you sitting there behind your stack of books—with your two posters. And dressed like an 1890s character.

You have to get their attention as they enter the store. Your garb, your posters, your little table with the sign on it that says "Author Signing Today" are all intended to help.

But selling is not a spectator sport. You have to take the initiative. Speak right up. Greet the customers as they come in the door, just as if you were a retiree moonlighting at the front door of Wal-Mart. One foolproof way to separate a prospect from a waste of time is to attempt to engage a customer entering the store in a conversation. Start out by saying something like, "Well, hello there. I've been waiting for you all afternoon. What took you so long?"

Now you have posed a personal question, one-on-one, that is clearly tongue-in-cheek. If the customer attempts to shrug it off and zip on by, let 'em go. They are never going to buy your book. Ever.

If, on the other hand, you get a smile back and an attempt at a quip in the way of an answer, chances are about one in five you can sell that person a book. Do not miss that twenty percent chance. Call them over to you. "Hey, c'mon over here. Check it out," as you wave them frantically toward your table with both arms.

Remember, your first job is to get a customer to come to you, to stop and engage. Simply inviting them, firmly, will almost always work—once they've noticed you.

Just try it. It's not only easy and fun, for you and most customers, but it also will immediately spike your opportunities to make sales.

Guaranteed.

Once they see you, engage them. One-on-one.

You have gotten the customer's attention. You invited them over with a tongue-in-cheek quip and a friendly wave. They're standing right in front of you, looking straight at you.

What in the world do you do now?

First, before you do anything else, without fail, every time—hand them a book. Get that product in their hands. Let them see it. Feel it. Open it. Fall in love with it. And then, as soon as they have taken possession of the book, ask a leading question that requires, or at least calls for, a response. For *Devil's Lust in the Dust Devils,* try something like, "Do you enjoy a good love story? One with a historic twist?" What you are attempting to do is to get them talking. Get them to say something that will give you a clue as to what they are looking for in a book.

If the answer is "I only read science fiction," you begin to politely get rid of that person. Immediately. Turn and point to where the science fiction books are, all the while saying, "You're not going to like my book then. Nothing scientific about it at all. But you'll find some really good ones over there."

Point is, you don't have time to waste with nonprospects.

If, on the other hand, the response has any smidgen of positive to it, go for the sale. Keep that person talking. Ask for a recent example of a book they have really enjoyed. Then tell them your book is quite similar, except it is a better story. And it's written better. As long as you keep smiling and maintain a twinkle in your eyes, you can get by with saying almost anything, no matter how outlandish it would seem out of context. But you are in context. So go for it.

Listen. And give that customer a reason to buy your book. Write that clause down on a three–by-five card and sleep on it, too: "Give that customer a reason to buy your book." A reason that is a direct response to something they have revealed to you—all in less than thirty seconds.

Yes, you can learn to do this. It's not hard. It just takes practice. *And remembering to listen.*

Separate the sheep from the goats. So to speak.

If your book appeals to women between twenty-five and forty-nine and to men over sixty-five, you should just forget about hailing and calling over everybody else. Right?

Not necessarily. A thirty-five-year-old male may be looking for a gift for his wife. Or his father. Casual visual discrimination—or profiling, as it's called in these days of PC—is not particularly reliable. It can cost you potential sales, even though failing to do it may waste a bit of your time. Since you are targeting between four and five sales an hour, you can afford to waste a half minute on a prospect at the risk of losing a sale.

"So," you are saying, "how is it that I decide who to approach?"

Here's the answer: Like almost any statistical universe, people who come into a bookstore fit very neatly into what I call the "prospects' bell curve." That is, about one in five is completely glassy-eyed. Completely oblivious to his or her surroundings. And at some point in his or her tragic life, has had a complete humorectomy. Absolutely no sense of humor whatsoever.

Forget about these people. They aren't going to buy your book. They just stopped in to go to the restroom. Or to have a cup of coffee. Or check out *Mechanix Illustrated.* I don't care what your book is about, they are not going to buy it. The good news is, it won't be too hard to avoid them, though.

Just don't stick out your foot and trip them, and they will pass on by. Let 'em go.

Now, about another one in five has twinkling eyes, a nice smile, a bouncing step.

Pay attention. Get ready. These folks are your best prospects.

Why?

Because they are smart, they are funny, they have a quick wit, and they will love bantering with you. Just long enough for you to hear something that will allow you to give them a reason to buy your book. But you have to really concentrate, because they are very, very quick. If they sense you're not up to their speed, they're outta there. Gone on to a bigger challenge than you have provided. So, sit on the edge of your chair, look right through their eyes into their brains, and be quick in replying to them. Do that, and you've just made a sale. I don't care if they are ninety years old and don't remember if they are male or female.

These intelligent types are pure gold.

And they frequent bookstores.

"Well," you say, "that still leaves the sixty percent in the middle." Right.

And some of them will be good prospects. Others won't. After you have sold a few dozen books (and paid attention to the kinds of people who are buying them), you will find it easier to sort out the buyers from the time-wasters in this vast middle group.

Meantime, it's okay to go first after the women twenty-five to forty-nine and the older gents.

By the way, this is a simple quintile analysis, in marketing terms. (Just in case you want to toss out that term to impress one of your haughty MBA acquaintances.)

Going for the jugular.

Let's talk a bit more about what to do when you have one of those people in front of you who is a bona fide prospect. One who has noticed you, reacted to your invitation, picked up your book and thumbed through it. Even asked you a couple of intelligent questions.

How do you set the hook?

Let them talk. As long as they are willing to stand there and converse, go with the flow. Because, as sure as God didn't make little green apples and it don't rain in Indianapolis—yada-yada-yada—that person is going to almost invite you to give him or her a reason to buy your book.

So listen. Respond. Ask questions.

Then listen some more. Pick up on the reason they're looking for—and then spring the trap. Give them that reason, followed immediately by a direct statement, such as, "You need this book. And I would be happy to sign it and personalize it for you right now. What is your name?"

Pick up your pen. Open a book. And get ready to sign.

Don't look up. Don't give that person any reason to pause. Just keep truckin' along. Nineteen times out of twenty, they will give you their name. Don't miss a beat. Ask immediately, "Do you spell that B-O-B?" Followed immediately by something like, "Don't laugh. I ran into a guy a couple of weeks ago who spelled it B-A-U-B."

Unless that person flees or screams, "Stop, you idiot!" just sign that book with his or her name on it and hand it to the customer with a warm smile and a big, "Thank you. I know you're going to love it."

Chi-n-n-n-g!

Ring up another sale.

You have listened to a potential customer with an obvious interest. You have given that customer a real reason to buy your book. You have personalized it, quickly, thus sealing the commitment.

And everybody wins. Not a thing wrong with that.

Just do it.

I do not mean to suggest that you ever use heavy-handed methods or take advantage of a customer. Either of those would likely violate the bookseller's canon of ethics, and you are, after all, a guest in their business establishment.

But in personal selling, the absence of a "no'" always means "yes."
Until you hear that "no," loud and clear, you've got a "yes." So, go for it.

A little ring-a-ding-ding never hurts.

You will occasionally run into a slow-decider, a potential customer who clearly has an interest in your book but one who is having a hard time articulating any reason to buy that you can feed back to them. When all else fails, bring out the showmanship.

Simply dressing up in period costume to match the setting of your book and being quick with a humorous, even outrageous quip—those do not constitute legitimate showmanship. So, teach yourself a simple sleight-of-hand magic trick. And arm yourself with some entertaining one-liners.

Win over that customer by being simply charming. Entertaining. Engaging.

Those who invariably have the hardest time deciding to plunk down their cash (or whip out their MasterCard) are the same folks who will buy the book because they "like you." They have a very subjective orientation—maybe even a total block against objectivity and even logic. But once they decide they "like" you, that you're an okay person, they're going to buy that book.

What have you done by employing a bit of showmanship? Nothing different from feeding back to the more objective, logical customers their own reasons to buy your book. You have just given these subjective types a reason to buy—on their own terms.

The eyes have it.

Finally, as you get more and more experience selling one-on-one, always taking care to keep your thinking fresh and your listening fine-tuned, you will find you can read the predisposition of a person to be a potential buyer by just looking into their eyes. Really!

Having done dozens of in-store signings, I have reached a point at which I can actually look into a customer's eyes and—with very few exceptions—tell if that customer is a red-hot prospect, a likely purchaser, a really hard sell, or a complete waste of my time.

I am sure I can't describe for you, writer though I am trying to be, how this is done. You learn it by experience. And every good salesman I have ever known will swear by it.

I didn't make it up. I just learned how to do it. By repetition.

You will, too. Without even thinking about it.

In fact, I want to encourage you not to think about it. Just let it happen.

Then one day, when you're re-reading this chapter, you will know what the hell I'm talking about.

Yes, you will.

Let's wrap it up.

I realize all these tips and instructions are a bit hard to circle the wagons around as you sit, wherever it is you are sitting, trying to imagine in your mind's eye the people and situations I have described in this chapter.

In fact, I wish I could personally visit every one of you who has bought this book. Take you with me to the sales floor of a major bookseller, and let you observe precise examples of what I have been describing in this chapter.

Since I can't do that, let me make an alternative suggestion: *Re-read this chapter after every book signing experience.*

You will immediately begin to relate these admittedly isolated examples to something—or someone—you have encountered that very day. And these tips will suddenly begin to become concrete and much more meaningful.

Keep re-reading it after every on-site selling experience until you believe you can enhance the examples with more of your own.

At that point, we will both know you've got the picture. For sure.

Good luck, my author friends.

¡Buena suerte!

Buona fortuna!

Or, as we say in Portuguese, *"E uma la plooma."*

Right?

"Hey, dudes! I'm here to sign some books."

Chapter 14: Where the Rubber Meets the Road.

Still Want To Be a Writer?
Good.

Crafting the message content of this book has been a big challenge from day one. Like walking a thin tightrope. Or running a gauntlet between good and evil. One on each side, don't you see?

As an author who has learned, often the hard way, what is expected of and required of us to successfully "move the tonnage," I knew I had to provide a straight dose of cold reality, represented by such potentially disheartening but absolutely factual statements as:

- You must simply learn how and take the lead role in selling your own book. Nobody else is going to do it for you. End of discussion.
- Publishers are beginning to look at manuscripts as "content" and authors as "content providers." We're all headed for Commoditysville.
- Most of us are never going to get rich or famous writing books.
- Booksellers don't owe us the time of day.
- You cannot edit and design your own book—and then expect to be able to sell it. Impossible. Ineffectual. Inadmissible.

In other words, if this book was going to be of real value to authors, I had to, in the irritating words of Howard Cosell, "Tell it like it is."

On the other hand, it was never my intent to discourage anyone from writing books, selling manuscripts—or trying to become rich and famous. Some of you will do just that. And good for you.

So I worked uncommonly hard (for a mostly lazy lout) to show you that it is possible—if not to count on becoming rich and famous, at least to maximize your chances of having some degree of success selling your book. That, too, is a dose of cold, hard reality.

But it's a positive reality.

My intent, then, was to share with you some of the tricks, shortcuts, and must-do's you will need to pay attention to if you are going to be more successful.

I thought briefly at one point—and quite casually—that I might have an advantage in delving into this subject because I am a trained and experienced (and successful) marketer of a wide variety of products and services—meat products, snack foods, soft drinks, consumer electronics whiz-bangs. But I didn't dwell on this point. Unfortunately.

I knew when I started down this road (to write books) that a book is both a product and a service. It is a product because it is something you can hold in your hand, put on a shelf, open and use. And it is a service because it represents many hours of entertainment, information, and even education for lots of people for many years to come.

If books are both products and services, I knew I could market them. The marketing disciplines for books are no different from those for banking, for soap powder, or beer, automobiles, or corn flakes. I knew how to and had great experience marketing these kinds of products and services.

The big difference, seemed to me, was that the makers of these products really want to sell them. To sell more and more every week. To max out the factory, and then build an addition to that factory. These makers have a burning desire to "move the tonnage."

But guess what?

Writers (many of them, anyway) didn't seem to me to share that desire—the wish to get in the trenches, duke it out with the competition, and develop the killer instinct it takes to be a successful marketer of anything.

And that puzzled me. I, not having been an author for more than a wink in time, just didn't get it. *What is wrong with these people?* I wondered to myself.

And I went right on doing, for my book, what I had learned to do and had done, with great success, for Pilgrim's Pride chicken, for Pepsi-Cola brands, for Wendy's Old Fashioned Hamburgers, for Cadillac and GTE and dozens of others over the years, from kilowatts to croutons, banks to broadcasters.

Just like I knew it would, it worked. Very quickly, I began to sell twenty to thirty copies (and more) of my book at almost any signing where there was moderate or better traffic. I learned that I could sell as many books in an hour (about four and one-half copies on the average), as most authors were selling at an entire signing.

I noticed that the good and talented people at my publisher quite often had difficulty communicating with and dealing with some other authors. I saw that they always responded positively to me, though.

And I wondered some more.

I saw that booksellers were always surprised—taken aback, even—by the volume of books I moved at a signing, as well as by the short-term follow on sales those signings produced. Invariably. I noticed that a couple of major chains had begun to come to me with offers to do signings—taken me under their massive wings. So to speak.

At big signing events, I heard many other authors complaining, sometimes bitterly and hatefully, that their publishers and the booksellers were doing "absolutely nothing" to sell their books.

And that got me to wondering even more. Because, in some cases, their publisher was my publisher. The bookstore chains they were lashing out at were the same ones that invited me back. Again and again.

Dimwit that I am sometimes, at first I just chalked the whole confusing phenomenon up to some lucky break. Or maybe my first book was just a helluva lot better than their books.

Fat chance.

It took an offhand observation from a very bright, young area marketing manager for one of the major chains to reveal to me a blinding flash of the obvious.

Epilogue: Still Want To Be a Writer? Good.

121

My only real advantage lay in the fact that I knew how to market—and how to sell, one-on-one.

Well, duh!

Suddenly, it all made sense. Most authors have never been exposed to the disciplines of marketing packaged goods. Or the ins-and-outs of dealing with CEOs at the boardroom level as a public relations counselor. They have never done retail store checks until the cows came home. Or learned to make French fries at Whataburger University.

Good heavens. I was truly blessed.

That young AMM's remark, to the effect that my experience made selling and understanding the entire process second nature to me, elicited a response. One of those unconsciously bright statements that sometimes just slip out, spontaneously, even though you do your best to pose as a dumb-butt.

I said something to the effect that good marketing is not black magic. It is neither hard nor complicated. But it requires planning, discipline, and desire to be effective. Then I went on to say, "I could teach any author to successfully market his or her books—provided that person really *wants* to be more successful. And is willing to stick to the plan and disciplines required."

These remarks were uttered without thinking. Didn't have to think about them. They are just facts. As sure as God didn't make little green yada-yada-yadas.

Fast forward one day.

Sipping my morning cup of coffee and doing my best to get my eyes open (after writing half the night, once again), I opened up my e-mailbox. There it was—the unexpected challenge.

The young AMM (also a marketing person, naturally) had thrown down the gauntlet: "What you said yesterday about teaching other authors an easy and simple marketing approach? That makes absolute sense. If you would write a how-to book for authors—how to market their books, including the roles of the publisher and the bookseller and everybody else involved—we [her chain] will work with you to sell it. Maybe we could even sponsor ninety-minute mini-seminars for writers. Right in our stores."

Hosanna! A golden opportunity for yours truly to accomplish

just about everything that's recommended in the preceding chapters. All in one little project.

So that is what I've tried to do here. After doing my homework. And talking to many authors, taking care to visit with both those who sit on their butts and complain bitterly (mostly because they don't know any better), as well as those whom I had observed doing a very credible and professional marketing job, whether by training and experience or by common-sense instinct.

I talked to everyone at Eakin Press, and I tried (with limited success) to get other publishers to talk about the subject. I also visited, briefly, with other AMMs and CRMs of bookstore chains and a couple of friends who own independent bookstores.

I found that everyone I talked to, other than authors, said exactly the same things. Clearly, there seemed to me to be a need.

So here it is. This book, I sincerely hope, has helped you—the author—to gain some insight into and the desire to participate in the mainstream of the marketing process.

If you will take it to heart, it will help you be more successful. Guaranteed.

And all for a measly $18.95. Plus tax.

Hallelujah!

Epilogue: Still Want To Be a Writer? Good.

123

Actual Research Results Report

Growing Up Simple
Reader Reaction Survey Results

Methodology: Twenty-four readers from across the U.S. agreed to read the manuscript and respond to a questionnaire. The questionnaire consists of ten separate seven-point semantic differential scales, five closed-end questions, and one completely open-ended question. The purpose of the questionnaire was to measure reactions to the book of a variety of individuals of differing ages and location, with approximately a 50-50 mix of male-female respondents.

Response Rate: Twenty-two of twenty-four readers polled returned the questionnaire, completed in total, giving a response rate of 91.67%—an acceptably high rate. Of the respondents, twelve are female and ten are male. Among them are approximately equal numbers of Great Depression Generation, In-Betweeners, and Baby Boomers. Three are members of Generation X.

Because the sample size is small, no attempt has been made to cross-tabulate except by gender.

Following are the results of the survey:

1. All things considered, my reaction to the book was:

	Female Respondents	Male Respondents	Total
Extremely positive	7	3	10
Very positive	5	6	11
Somewhat positive	-	-	-
No opinion	-	-	-
Somewhat negative	-	-	-
Very negative	-	-	-
Extremely negative	-	-	-
Totals	**12**	**9**	**21**

Analysis: Clearly the book is overwhelmingly considered quite positive by the respondents. Females tended to rank it slightly more positively than males.

Comment: This response set is, indeed, good news to the author. I had concern the book might not appeal to women. Wrong!

2. I found the book to be:

	Female Respondents	Male Respondents	Total
Extremely interesting	7	3	10
Very interesting	5	6	11
Somewhat interesting	-	-	-
No opinion	-	-	-
Somewhat uninteresting	-	-	-
Very uninteresting	-	-	-
Extremely uninteresting	-	-	-
Totals	**12**	**9**	**21**

Analysis: Clearly, the book is considered quite interesting, again with females ranking it slightly higher than males. Note that the responses are identical to question one, although individual responses are not identical.

3. For me, the book was:

	Female Respondents	Male Respondents	Total
Extremely entertaining	8	4	12
Very entertaining	4	5	9
Somewhat entertaining	-	-	-
No opinion	1	-	1
A little bit boring	-	-	-
Very boring	-	-	-
Extremely boring	-	-	-
Totals	**13**	**9**	**22**

Analysis: The positive trend continues, as does the trend toward slightly higher rankings by women than men. Respondents found the book highly entertaining. The one "no opinion" notation was actually just left blank, entirely.

Comment: The primary intent of the book, from the author's point-of-view, is to entertain. Apparently it has succeeded. The combination of high marks for entertainment, interest, and positive reaction are heartening.

4. In my estimation, the book is:

	Female Respondents	Male Respondents	Total
Extremely informative	3	1	4
Very informative	5	5	10
Somewhat informative	3	3	6
No opinion	-	-	-
Somewhat uninformative	-	-	-
Very uninformative	-	-	-
Completely uninformative	-	-	-
Totals	**11**	**9**	**20**

Analysis: Respondents found the book informative, but to a lesser degree than the previous three measurements. Again, women found it slightly more informative than men.

Comment: These rankings are, indeed, a pleasant surprise, since there was never any real intent on the author's part to inform the reader.

5. I think the book is:

	Female Respondents	Male Respondents	Total
Hilarious	5	2	7
Very funny	6	6	12
A little bit humorous	1	1	2
No opinion	-	-	-
A little bit dull	-	-	-
Very dull	-	-	-
Extremely dull	-	-	-
Totals	**12**	**9**	**21**

Analysis: Respondents overwhelmingly found the book to contain a high level of humor. Once again, female readers considered it a bit more humorous than male readers.

Comment: If entertainment is the objective of the book, humor is the strategy to entertain. The strategy seems to be working well.

6. For my taste, the book is:

	Female Respondents	Male Respondents	Total
Way too short	1	1	2
Fairly short	2	4	6
Somewhat abbreviated	-	3	3
Correct length	9	1	10
Somewhat lengthy	-	-	-
Fairly long	-	-	-
Way too long	-	-	-
Totals	**12**	**9**	**21**

Analysis: Here we see the first significant deviation from consensus.

While approximately half the readers see the book as the right length, the other half ranked it on the short side.

Comment: At 65,000 words, the book—in fact—is not short. Rather, it is about an average-size book. The average reader will require between 5.75 and 7.25 hours to read the entire book. There may be several reasons for the "short" appearance. First, readers received the manuscript chapter-by-chapter over approximately a twelve-week period. They professed to want to read a lot more (see below) and apparently anticipated the next installment in most instances. Too, many indicated that the book was "easy to read." All these factors may have combined to leave the reader with the perception that the book is short.

7. *When I finished the book, I:*

	Female Respondents	Male Respondents	Total
Wanted to read a lot more	6	3	9
Wanted to read some more	5	4	9
Wanted to read a little more	1	1	2
No opinion	-	1	1
Was glad it was over	-	-	-
Was very glad it was over	-	-	-
Was ecstatic I was finished	-	-	-
Totals	**12**	**9**	**21**

Analysis: Respondents professed to want to read more after having read the entire book. Again, female respondents were somewhat more predisposed to read-on than male.

Comment: Every entertainer and every writer strives to "leave 'em wanting more." Apparently that phenomenon is at work among these readers.

8. If the same author wrote another book, I:

	Female Respondents	Male Respondents	Total
Definitely would read it	11	7	18
Probably would read it	1	1	2
Might read it	-	1	1
Not sure	-	-	-
Might not read it	-	-	-
Probably wouldn't read it	-	-	-
Definitely wouldn't read it	-	-	-
Totals	**12**	**9**	**21**

Analysis: Respondents overwhelmingly want to read more by this author.

Comment: A second book in a similar style, but with an entirely different story to tell, is at the outline stage. A good marketing strategy ought to be a one-two punch, with the second book ready to be released when sales of the first book crest.

9. In thinking about this book as a gift I might give someone, I would:

	Female Respondents	Male Respondents	Total
Definitely give it	8	5	13
Probably give it	3	2	5
Might give it	1	2	3
Don't know	-	-	-
Might not give it	-	-	-
Probably not give it	-	-	-
Definitely not give it	-	-	-
Totals	**12**	**9**	**21**

Analysis: Respondents show a high propensity to think of the book as a gift item.

Comment: The response bodes well for multiple sales to single individuals. Maybe a May "graduation" gift promotion?

10. *If this book were available in a bookstore in hardback, I would expect to pay:*

	Female Respondents	Male Respondents	Total
$10 to $15	2	2	4
$15 to $20	7	4	11
$21 to $25	3	3	6
More than $25	-	-	-
No response	1	-	1
Totals	**13**	**9**	**22**

Analysis: Most respondents seem to think the book should sell for more than $15, but less than $25, with a cluster at the $19.95 price point.

Comment: Likely more research needs to be done on price point. The author believes that, maybe, the perceived "shortness" of the book may have skewed the price perception downward, artificially. Since perception is more important than fact, however, it may be necessary to add two to three chapters to the early part of the book. That would not be too difficult, but the author wants to be sure any additions are relevant and not just "padding."

11. My three favorite chapters were:

Chapter Number &Title	Female Respondents	Male Respondents	Total
2. You're Too Little	6	4	10
5. Folks See What They . . .	2	4	6
12. Two for the Road	3	2	5
1-16. Liked/loved them all	**3**	**1**	**4**
3. Pyromania and Kidnapping	-	3	3
4. Nifty New Flying . . .	-	3	3
6. What Goes Around . . .	2	1	3
7. Money Laundering	1	2	3
8. Dangling Participles	2	1	3
11. Grapefruit Heard 'Round . . .	3	-	3
10. Stepping Up to the Big . . .	1	1	2
13. Looking for Love in All . . .	-	2	2
1. It Was a Dark and Stormy . . .	1	-	1
9. Life's Hard When You're . . .	1	-	1
14. Trouble in River City . . .	1	-	1
16. Growing Up Simple	-	1	1
15. Running Flat-Out	-	-	0
Totals	**26**	**25**	**51**

Comment: Chapter 2 is a runaway favorite. Likewise, chapters 5 and 12 seem to be favored. It is interesting to note that every chapter except 15 (Running Flat-Out) received at least one mention as a favorite. That indicates that there must be something for almost anybody. Also heartening is the significant number of respondents who blew off the questionnaire and wrote in their own answer—they "liked" or "loved" all the chapters. Note that Chapter 15 (see below) was also not mentioned once as a "least liked" chapter.

12. *The three chapters I liked least were:*

Chapter Number &Title	Female Respondents	Male Respondents	Total
Liked/loved all of them	**8**	**4**	**12**
6. What Goes Around . . .	1	2	3
8. Dangling Participles	3	-	3
9. Life's Hard When You're . . .	1	2	3
10. Stepping Up to the Big . . .	1	2	3
3. Pyromania and Kidnapping	1	1	2
11. Grapefruit Heard 'Round . . .	1	1	2
14. Trouble in River City . . .	1	1	2
16. Growing Up Simple	1	1	2
1. It Was a Dark and Stormy . . .	-	1	1
2. You're Too Little	-	1	1
4. Nifty New Flying . . .	-	1	1
5. Folks See What They . . .	-	1	1
7. Money Laundering	-	1	1
12. Two for the Road	-	-	0
13. Looking for Love in All . . .	-	-	0
15. Running Flat-Out	-	-	0
Totals	**18**	**19**	**37**

Comment: More than half the respondents chose to write in that they "loved" or "liked" all the chapters and would not/could not identify any as "liked least." That is remarkable. And gratifying. Reaction to Chapter 8 (Dangling Participles) among women was anticipated, but on a much larger scale. Apparently nothing would be too gross for 75% of the female respondents. It is also interesting to note that a significantly larger proportion of male respondents were willing to list a "least liked" chapter. I have no explanation for this phenomenon, except, perhaps, that women feel less compelled to color within the lines.

13. If I were to compare this book to any other book(s) I have ever read, I think it most resembles:

Male Responses

Author	Book	Number of Mentions
James Thurber	*My Life and Hard Times*	1
J. D. Salinger	*Catcher in the Rye*	1
Mark Twain	*Huckleberry Finn*	1
Mark Twain	*Tom Sawyer*	1
James Herriot	*All Creatures Great & Small*	1
Jean Shepherd	*Wanda Hickey's Night of Golden Memories*	1
Peter Gent	*The Last Magic Summer*	1
	Unlike anything I've ever read/unique	3
	Totals	**10**

Female Responses

Author	Book	Number of Mentions
John Irving	*A Prayer for Owen Meany*	1
John Irving	*The World According to Garp*	1
Garrison Keillor	(Anything by Keillor)	2
Harper Lee	*To Kill a Mockingbird*	1
Clyde Edgerton	*Walking Across Egypt*	1
Robert Fulghum	*Anything I Ever Needed to Know I Learned . . .*	1
Rick Bragg	*All Over But the Shouting*	1
Nicholas Sparks	*The Notebook*	1
	Tuesdays With Morrie	1
	Divine Secrets of the YaYa Sisterhood	1
	Unlike anything I've ever read/unique	4
	Totals	**15**

Comment: Wow! Almost all the authors/books listed are American classics. To be placed in this kind of company is both gratifying and a bit frightening. For lack of a better explanation, the author will take the results as a supreme compliment and simply say, "Thank you."

All the books/authors listed seem to have one thing in common. The books are stories told by storytellers. That is what the author has sought to do with *Growing Up Simple.* Just tell a story in an engaging, entertaining fashion.

14. Three things I would do to improve the book:

Suggestion	Number of Mentions	Author's Comment
Include photos, maps, headlines/items of the day	3	Will use both photos and illustrations
Fewer/eliminate "Heh-heh"	3	Done
Too critical of parents	2	But truthful
Make the book longer	2	Why? Possible, but to what purpose?
Include more anecdotes	1	Several added
Use "lagniappe" less	1	Fixed
"Commenced to" overused	1	Sure was. Mostly removed.
Make stories longer	1	Have made several longer.
More detailed descriptions	1	Done
Use "anal" less	1	Done. Now used only once.
More teen romance detail/description	1	Chapters 13, 16 rewritten to fix.
More about family in later chapters	1	Nothing much to tell.
Be sure language fits period	1	Great catch. All fixed.
Identify henchpersons better up front	1	Before they enter story?
Develop henchpersons more	1	Worked on it.
Reduce unpleasant words after Chapter 2	1	Sorry, but that's the vernacular of the day.
Make "In-Betweener" connection more clear	1	Good point. Will fix.
Get somebody famous to write foreword	1	How about Liz Carpenter? I'm trying to get her.
Nothing. Ready "as is."	**4**	Thanks, but . . .

Comment: These suggestions, criticisms have been immensely helpful. Not all of them can be accommodated, but many of them have helped make the book much, much better. I thank each of the respondents for their thoughtful insights.

15. As far as believability goes, I found the book:

	Female Respondents	Male Respondents	Total
Totally believable	5	2	7
Mostly believable	7	7	14
A little bit believable	-	-	-
Don't know	-	-	-
A little bit unbelievable	-	-	-
Mostly unbelievable	-	-	-
Totally unbelievable	-	-	-
Totals	**12**	**9**	**21**

Comment: Every storyteller strives to make his or her audience "believe." Clearly, this group of respondents found the stories in *Growing Up Simple* to be believable. As the verbatim comments (below) and notations in the margins of the questionnaire report, younger readers had some trouble believing the freedom the author's group of friends had to pursue mischief.

And that is one of the major points of the book; i.e., that times were simpler. Safer. Less threatening. Children today, with that kind of freedom, would likely get into trouble, big time. Not because they are any different from their parents or grandparents, but because their environment has become much, much more hostile. For In-Betweeners, sneaking a beer would equate to shooting up with heroin today. The stakes are higher today, and the consequences geometrically more devastating. So sad.

16. Verbatim: Is there anything else you would like to say about the book?

Female Responses

"It was an engaging trip through a more innocent time, led by a charming scalawag whose wit, independence and intelligence made the reader want to know him better and count on him as [a] friend."

—In-Betweener

"It puts the reader directly in the time and place. It's a very personal look-see, on-the-scene visit. It has such a personal style that it gives a feeling of hearing a friend tell about his experiences. I think that's what all writers strive for."

—Great Depression Generation

"I wish I could have done some of the things you did. Your escapades sound like so much fun."

—Great Depression Generation

"Takes us all back to our childhoods."

—In-Betweener

"This book conjured up so many wonderful memories, things I hadn't thought about in years and years."

—In-Betweener

"You and your friends were an unbelievable group! You guys were wild, crazy, uninhibited. How many kids meet the President of the United States?"

—In-Betweener

"I found it only a little bit believable until I talked to other people your age. Then I believed most of it."

—Baby Boomer

"Had a hard time deciding my favorite chapters. LOVED reading the book."

—Baby Boomer

"Certain stories were really touching and others were remarkably funny. I made other people listen to me retelling some of your stories."

—In-Betweener

"This would be a great movie!"
—Generation X

"I loved the 'Life's Lesson's Learned' at the end of each chapter."
—Great Depression Generation

"You are a talented writer, and your style is very friendly and easy to read. Almost like you're right there telling the story. That's the major charm of the book."
—In-Betweener

"Your 'apology' in Chapter 11 is just one example of how you are able to turn incidents into laugh-out-loud humor. There's humor throughout that is delightful, and some is beautifully subtle. But it's always there."
—Great Depression Generation

"The plot gets an A+ for originality. I believe it will SELL BIG. To all ages and types. It's non-fiction that reads like a novel."
—Great Depression Generation

Male Responses

"You've got to publish it. It's hilarious! It's the best coming-of-age book I've seen since (J.D.) Salinger's Catcher in the Rye.*"*
—In-Betweener

"I loved it. This is one of the funniest and most true-to-life books I've read in a long time."
—In-Betweener

"It was fun for me to read and share your growing up experiences."
—Great Depression Generation

"This is one of the most enjoyable books I have ever read."
—Great Depression Generation

"I would buy it. Maybe even pay retail."
—Baby Boomer

"I like your style and your ability to create 'word pictures' that bring the reader into the story."
—Great Depression Generation

"The reader can easily relate to the characters and become friends with them. It is the kind of book that makes you sorry to come to the end."
—Great Depression Generation

"You and your group play out the protagonist/antagonist roles well. The epilogue is good. Do you still have a 'crush' on Mary Lee?"
—Great Depression Generation

P.S.—Although the numbers of sub-group respondents are too small to make any statistical conclusions meaningful, the responses of the In-Betweener readers, true to form, stand out as comparable to one another, but different from all the others. In-Betweeners remain contrarians to the end.
—George Arnold

Appendix: Actual Research Results Report.

A Useful Guide to Words, Phrases, and Buzzwords of the Publishing Industry
(That Every Author Needs to Know, Understand, and Use)

authoritis: A debilitating condition, characterized by severe pains in the neck that progress rapidly downward to the buttocks. Commonly suffered by publishers, book designers, booksellers, and editors. Caused by authors' constant whining and massive egos.

beback: What nineteen out of twenty potential buyers will say once they've decided not to buy your book. "I'll be back." Don't believe it. It's a lie.

bestseller: (*referring to books*) A book which sells hundreds of thousands of copies, if not millions of copies; (*referring to people*) What every author should want to be called after a bookstore signing session. "She's a bestseller at our store." That will require selling four to five books an hour and working six to eight hours. Minimum. But you can do it. Yes, you can!

book designers: The talented, artistic people at your publisher who will make beautiful, tasty lemonade from the sack of lemons you call a manuscript. And crack you over the head with a swivel chair if you are too helpful—in an artistic way.

bozo: A name you do not want to earn among publishers, editors, book designers, AMMs, CRMs, or anybody else, for that matter. Refers to those "out-to-lunch" types who just won't pay attention to anybody or anything except the secret voices within their own heads. Seemingly.

condomidioms: Words and phrases, commonly employed by authors, that are so hidden and obscure in the everyday lexicon as to be unknown by more than 99 and 44/100 percent of all potential readers. Often marked by editors with the term "Say *what?*"

doofus: The kindest moniker applied to authors by various others in the chain of producing and successfully selling books—publishers, booksellers, editors, book designers, publishers' sales reps, area marketing managers, community relations managers, inventory managers, and bookstore general managers. Be proud to be a doofus. Seek that status. As opposed to an arrogant #!★@head, dweeb, chicken%$&#, @#★&#!, or %@★&!#. All of which are worse. But cleverly descriptive. Easily understood. Picturesque. And often precise.

editor: The person who will fix all your misteaks, faux pas'es, mispelings, factual errers, continuity lapses, repetition, dangling participles, repetition, punctuation; misplaced modifiers, and downright stupidities. (My editor took a coffee break to help me demonstrate this point.) If you are respectful and cooperative. Or, if you are not respectful and cooperative, ignore a few of them so as to show the world what an ignorant ass you really are. Be very nice to this person. The reputation you save may be your own.

fun: Stuff you'd better have a lot of in this business of writing and selling books – in lieu of making a potful of money. Which you probably won't.

get-up: The ridiculous outfit you may put on for a bookstore signing or event appearance to draw attention to yourself—to get noticed and grab a potential book buyer's attention.

hysterical fiction: Any official report or study commissioned by a government body, written by a committee, or researched and reported by a bunch of church ladies. Of any denomination, creed, or particular dogma.

humorectomy: Voluntary or involuntary procedure resulting in the absence of any sense of humor, whatsoever, in the process of writing, publishing, editing, and selling books. Commonly displayed by approximately twenty percent (lowest quintile) of all shoppers in any given bookstore. At any time. (Yes, I know the two H's are not correctly alphabetized. Did you catch that mistake? If you didn't, don't try to be an editor. Please.)

independent: Any bookstore not owned and operated by a major bookseller chain. Also, a condition which a particularly obnoxious author may acquire after being abandoned by a frustrated editor, banned from a publisher's offices, and hit over the head with a swivel chair by a thoroughly justified book designer. Synonym: On your own, butthead.

jackshit: The sum of all knowledge apparently possessed by many authors when it comes to understanding publishing, editors, book designers, booksellers, and the need to participate, actively, in the process of marketing their own books.

kaput: Old German idiom. This is what an author will be after refusing, steadfastly, to participate in the process of selling his or her own book. Italian equivalent—*e finito.* In Spanish—*al fin.* In Portuguese— *e uma la plooma.*

last time: Time continuum description of a bookseller's future propensity to invite an author back to participate in another signing if that author is not respectful, cooperative, and capable of selling his or her own books. Really.

marketing plan: An author's job to develop and put into practice. See Part IV, Chapters 9 through 11. Or get a good-paying union job on an assembly line. And burn your word processing software.

never again: See "last time" above.

next time: Booksellers' code words for the back corner, among the tomes on marital problems, where you will be placed if they ever do forget and invite you back again for another signing —if you're not much into cooperating and selling your own book.

oxymoron: Label used to describe the term "finished manuscript." Also spelled Oxy-Moron, a patent-medicine skin cream applied topically to clear up your brain and improve your intelligence quotient (IQ).

personal selling: What every author who wants to be a bestseller has to learn to do. Even if it means becoming someone else who can better handle rejection. It's okay to do that. Be somebody else, that is. Such as one of the characters in your book, maybe?

publisher: Whoever pays (springs for the money) to have a manuscript printed and distributed. In addition, the people who will lock you out of their offices, after tossing your manuscript onto the lawn out front, if you become too obnoxious.

quintile analysis: The process of dividing any universe into five equally sized components for further study or analysis—such as all the shoppers in a bookstore on any given day. Also, the number of pieces an author can be expected to be carved into by his or her editor, book designer, AMM, CRM, and/or publisher if that author just doesn't "get it." Following painful and protracted evisceration. In addition, a term with which to impress your haughty MBA acquaintances. Those you would like to eviscerate. Go ahead. Admit it.

respect: Something every author must accumulate in abundance. And disseminate indiscriminately to every other person in the process of publishing and selling his or her book. Or reside forever in publishing infamy.

selling: Something you have now learned how to do. Learned you must do. Learned you cannot escape doing. Unless you want to be shunned by booksellers, languish in complete obscurity, remain penniless, have sand kicked in your face on the beach by muscle-bound bullies, suffer the slings and arrows of outrageous fortune. Are you getting the point? Good. Just do it.

typo: Commonly used short version of "typographical error." More common use in the book trade: "That author's some type o' idiot." Or, "She's the type o' writer who thinks all she has to do is finish a manuscript." Do not become a type o'. Or a typo.

uma la plooma: All-purpose string of syllables that can be passed off as meaning virtually anything in Portuguese. Who would know? Or care?

viagras: The closest thing in existence to magic pixie dust. Substances that may help you get up the nerve to be your own marketer and salesperson. So to speak.

Watch out!: A phrase commonly shouted by someone remote from the actual proximity in which a completely justified book designer has raised a swivel chair over his or her head in preparation for sending a know-it-all author to the infirmary. Or the great beyond. Pay attention. It may keep you from suffering a compound fracture. And shorten your stay in intensive care.

X-rated: A term that can be applied to the front cover of your book if you *really* want it to be bought and read by church ladies. Or Christian-right ministers.

yo mama: Your most severe critic. Also, perhaps the only person who will truly think your manuscript deserves to be a book. Or at least will profess to think so. Even if she really thinks it stinks.

zero: Aggregate sum of all the net monies an author's book will earn if that author is not willing to participate, actively and appropriately, in the processes of marketing and selling. Guaranteed. Synonym: zip.

——— Acknowledgments ———

A number of people provided me with invaluable assistance in the writing of this book. I am indebted to each of them:

■ To Jennifer Brown, area marketing manager for Borders Books, not only for having the creativity to suggest that I write this book, but also for the valuable input she provided from a bookseller's point of view. And also for having the trust to give me a shot at signings. We have sold a lot of books together. Thanks, Jennifer.

■ To all my friends at Eakin Press—Virginia and Tom Messer, heads of production and sales, to Amber Stanfield, the best little book designer east of West Overshoe, to Melissa Roberts, a precise and creative editor, and the entire supporting cast. You're the best.

■ To my author friend, Linda Bingham, who provided a great deal of input and information on what's already out there on this subject, as well as being a role model of an author who knows how to market her own books. Very well.

■ To my other author friend, Nancy McCoy, who writes like I think, says a lot of things I wish I had said, and practices a little serious law on the side. So to speak. Thanks, Nancy.

■ To my brother and sister-in-law, Jim and Barbara Arnold, for agreeing to wade through the manuscript of a how-to book on a subject completely foreign to both of them, catching mistakes and making great suggestions for improvement. *Gracias.*

■ To my friend, business partner, and sales consultant, Ken Squier, who can sell ice cubes to Siberians, and who has trained more than one great sales force. Thanks, Killer.

■ To my multi-talented friend, Lynn Adler—singer, songwriter, author, editor—for catching and fixing the biggest marketing gaffe since New Coke. And giving this book both a thorough once-over and a title that will turn heads.

■ To my Italian wife, Mary, for allowing me to work half the night and portray her in this book as someone she definitely is not. *Grazie, mi amore.*

To each of these people I extend my sincere gratitude. All the mistakes in this book are mine and mine alone. [Editor's note: Ain't he great?] If you find anything about it that you don't like, it's probably because I ignored the advice of someone cleverer than I.

—— About the Author ——

Photo: Terry Collier

George Arnold started writing his first book at age fifty-eight, sold it on the first submission he prepared, and has marketed it successfully, using the knowledge he gained in his thirty-two-year career as a marketing, advertising, sales promotion and public relations practitioner. "Just doing what I would do with any quality product," he says.

He retired in 1999 and lives in the Texas Hill Country with his wife of forty years. They raise registered Half-Arabian horses, dogs, cats, BB English Red bantams, and invisible goats. Yes, they do.

His first book, *Growing Up Simple . . . In Texas,* was winner of the coveted 2003 Silver Spur Award for excellence in marketing planning and execution, awarded by the Texas Public Relations Association, and the "IPPY" Humor Award for funniest book of 2003, presented by the Independent Publishers Book Awards. *Bestseller* is his third book.